SAMPRAS

A legend
in the works

SAMPRAS

A legend in the works

An unauthorised look at one of the most misunderstood tennis giants of all time

H.A. BRANHAM

Foreword by
BUD COLLINS

The Breedon Books
Publishing Company
Derby

First published in the United States of America in 1996 by Bonus Books Inc of 160 East Illinois Street, Chicago, Illinois 60611.
This edition first published in the United Kingdom in 1997 by The Breedon Books Publishing Company Ltd of 44 Friar Gate, Derby, England.

ISBN 1 85983 076 5

Printed by Butler & Tanner Ltd, Frome, Somerset, England.

Colour separations by RPS Ltd, Leicester, England.

Jackets printed by Lawrence-Allen, Weston-super-Mare, Avon, England.

Contents

For Cathie and the kids – Lee, Patrick, Austin and Alexis —
and the rest of my family. And for my late Uncle Freddy, a
Columbian clay-courter of minimal skill but grand foresight,
who thought a tennis racquet was a good present for a 12-year-old,
knowing that with the racquet, the kid would get the sport's joys
as part of the deal.

Acknowledgments

IN ANY SORT of undertaking such as this, benefactors of varying types and degrees surface, either by design or by luck, all contributing in some way to the finished product. I therefore would be remiss if I neglected to mention the following who, in no particular order, must indeed be judged benefactors:

P.C. Smith, my sports editor at the *Tampa Tribune,* whose go-ahead was prompted by the thought of me being out of the country for an extended period, but whose support was unwavering. Well, almost unwavering. But it was absolutely invaluable, in any case.

Media colleagues Bud Collins, Pete Bodo, Sandra Harwitt, Mark Winters and Paul Fein — who provided help through the spoken and written word and those others who helped via encouragement.

Photographer Cynthia Lum, whose eye speaks volumes with each snap of the shutter.

The tireless staff in the ATP Tour communications department, one Greg Sharko in particular.

The USTA communications department, especially Randy Walker, Art Campbell and Page Crosland, whose help in a variety of ways was invaluable.

Barbara Travers at the International Tennis Federation.

Rod Laver, who graciously shared his time and his perspectives.

The Walsh family, whose weeks of summer solitude on Britain's southern coast proved essential to this task.

The makers of Blackthorn's Dry Cider, who must be lauded for curing a series of writer's blocks along the way.

And finally, Pete Sampras, who has been nothing but a friend throughout the last three years, while at the same time being a joy to watch and write about.

Thanks to one, to all. Cheers.
H.A. Branham

Foreword

I F KEATS, the champion poet — surely you remember his *Ode on a Grecian Urn?* — were still around, he would doubtless be a communicant at Wimbledon. Sitting in Centre Court, amid roses, hydrangeas and the ghosts of illustrious world conquerors, he would be inspired to salute Sampras, the champion player, with 'Ode on an Earnest Greek'.

Keats would be stuck by the rural Hellenic features, the Olympian grace and poetic movement. He might summon images of a latter-day Zeus launching thunderbolts at foes while maintaining an unruffled mien. Totally carried away, would he dub Sampras' compelling rhythms as Pete's Peerless Pentameter? A little unlikely for Keats. But maybe he would recycle or paraphrase a couple of his old 'Urn' lines:

> Fair youth, beneath the trees,
> What leaf-fringed legend haunts
> About thy shape of deities or mortals
> Or of both?
> What man or god is this?
> What mad pursuit? What struggle to escape?
> What wild ecstasy!

Of course, the earnest Sampras is mortal. Nevertheless he's one of a fortunate, gifted few able to perform like a god. So fluid, almost languid, in his mad pursuit for lasting greatness, he struggles to escape the claws of rivals and achieve the ecstasy of the biggest-sounding, smallest figure: No.1.

Wouldn't Keats have loved Sampras? I'm not so sure the reverse would be true, but who knows? Whatever, Pete Sampras and John Keats, prodigies at their arts, will last as long as people care about tennis and poetry.

Each cut an indelible swathe early. Keats died at 26 in Rome. Sampras had some uncomfortable moments there, too, although at 23 he was a rare American guy in mastering the salmon-hued soil of Il Foro Italico to win the Italian Open. But five years before, when I encountered him at Il Foro in 1989, he was a homesick teenager longing for a fix of American junk food. "This is Sampras?" I asked myself.

Because he wasn't the kid I'd had been introduced to in the US Open locker room at Flushing Meadow two years earlier. Same good smile, but he'd seemed a midget among the junior competitors then, upwardly unspurted. In 1989, instead of sitting in a high school classroom he was furthering his tennis education, making the grand tour as it used to be called, getting his brains scrambled in alien studies: continental clay in Rome and Paris, followed by the capricious grass of Wimbledon. Still, it wasn't all Fs on the report card. He and pal Jim Courier did pull off one unexpected A-plus. They won the Italian Doubles title, the youngest pair to do so.

But Pete didn't dig the dirt. Since it took years before he reached a point of not quite detesting clay, it would have been preposterous to even imagine Pete as the US Open champion merely 16 months later. And I didn't. Somehow, though, the preposterous happened.

I had only hoped and yearned for a champion of his nature. In time his bearing, his lanky, loose-limbed flow, power and even temper made Pete seem a throwback to two other exemplary Californians, the earlier, long-trousered Ellsworth Vines and Don Budge.

Because he was such a good, friendly, unassuming kid riding a sweet style and a sporting demeanour that also evoked the old Aussies he admired, Rod Laver and Ken Rosewall, I hoped that some day he would transform obvious talent into championships. Obvious talent at striking the ball, but there has to be more. Much more.

I recall my friend, Gianni Clerici, as sharp a tennis critic as you'll find, rhapsodising about Sampras after watching him play Michael Chang in the US Open Juniors at Flushing. "His moves, his touch, he reminds me of Manolo Santana," said Clerici, who writes for the Roman daily, *La Repubblica*. High praise from a man not given to gushing. Bringing the magical Spaniard, Santana, winner of Wimbledon, French and US titles during the 1960s, into the conversation meant he'd been genuinely impressed.

But, as Gianni would admit, his appraisal was brief and superficial. You can't inspect the insides of a splendid stylist, measure the heart and head, the guts, the temperament.

Nikki Pilic, one of the best players to come out of the former Yugoslavia, and now the German Davis Cup captain, is suspicious when he hears somebody described as an exceptional talent on the basis of an array of brilliant strokes. "Talent is more than hitting the ball and moving well. I'm sick of hearing about guys who had the greatest strokes in the world, could have been champions if they'd felt like it," Pilic snorts. "Feeling like it, even when you don't feel like it — that's talent. It is being able to travel all the time, accept poor conditions and losing while you learn. It is fighting, sticking with it when you're playing bad.

"For me, a European," he laughs, "it was getting used to the lousy food in the United States, being with people who don't speak your language and look down on you because you don't speak theirs. There's more to being a professional than playing points and matches. Can you get through the discouragement of loneliness, homesickness, injuries, the times you've choked? If you can stick around out here, earn a living, want it bad enough — shut out everything on the big points but winning them — that's talent."

Amen.

I thought of Ion Tiriac. Tiriac, the hulking erstwhile Romanian Davis Cupper who managed the young Wimbledon-winning Boris Becker, is a wealthy entrepreneur who keeps a finger in tennis. "I am the best tennis player who cannot play tennis," Tiriac used to say, and you would agree, puzzled that a guy with the strokes of a Parisian street sweeper could do so well. Grotesque, but gritty, grubbing and grasping, he had the right talent, all right, the talent of wanting it so badly — a hunger — that he beat most opponents, including his betters when they didn't pay strict attention.

One sultry September afternoon at Flushing Meadow ('Flushing Toilets' is Tiriac's term, not of endearment), I first felt that Pete Sampras had that kind of insatiable hunger-talent embedded beneath the electrifying whip of his shot-making.

Everything was working as he won the first two sets of a 1990 quarter-final against Ivan Lendl. This was still Lendl the giant, a hard-edged guy who had appeared in a Tilden-tying record of eight consecutive US finals (winning in 1985-86-87). And when Ivan rebounded to take the next two sets, and Pete's head drooped — a mannerism that may yet call for posture lessons — other heads, in the press box, shook knowingly. The chance appeared gone because this was Ivan Lendl in a fifth set of the US Open. "Nice try, kid. Maybe next time."

What we knowers didn't know: Sampras was ready to make history. He straightened up and removed Lendl as a contender. My head was nodding "Yes!" now, and I said to John Feinstein, "Nobody beats Pete in this tournament." Feinstein, who was trailing Pete's progress for vignettes in his book, *Hard Courts*, nodded, too, agreeing enthusiastically.

The rest, beating up on two crowd favourites, John McEnroe and Andre Agassi, though fun to behold, seemed almost anti-climactic. The victory over Lendl, having to retool for the fifth set — the 15th round against an all-time heavyweight champ — punched the kismet button for me. That want-it-need-it talent was on display.

Knocking out favoured Agassi, 6-4, 6-3, 6-2, for the title, Pete overtook a guy he'd never heard of — but who had? — Oliver Campbell. A century before, Campbell, a New Yorker, was the youngest of US champions at 19 years, five months. Pete, the high school dropout, undercut the Columbia graduate by four months.

The game had changed a little bit since 1890. Campbell, a true-blue amateur, won on the grass of the Newport (R.I.) Casino, defended his title successfully in 1891-92, then retired at age 21; his old man suggested that it was time to go to work. Sampras, entering the labour force as a pro at 17, and soon enough a millionaire, was still learning his business when he was 21, learning that one US championship on the mean green slabs of Flushing did not qualify anyone for sporting canonisation.

Pete got rich in 1990. He followed up on the US Open title by seizing the $2 million first prize in the hastily and unnecessarily thrown-together Grand Slam Cup. Although it was a contrived event, crafted to upstage the year-ending ATP Championship — serving only to further confuse tennis followers — the money was real, and Sampras grabbed it.

Thereupon followed an interesting period of adjustment to a new-found romance — with the bitch goddess, Fame. Pete went a touch daffy. Serious money for exhibitions hung from vines everywhere, like luscious bunches of grapes, and he plucked feverishly, understandably distracted and losing sight of what he was about: major titles. One trouble was he kept getting hurt while diving for dollars in make-believe matches and had to pull out of the 1991 Australian Open.

A concerned friend, encountering him a month later —at Palm Springs, asked, "Pete, why do you risk injury in exos? How much money do you need? A lot of us believe that if you concentrate on what really counts you could be a great player."

"Could be?" His thick black brows twitched, his dark eyes blazed disdainfully at a perceived put-down, and he stalked off, curtly dismissing an act of *lèse majesté*. "Could be?"

He'd had a great US Open, true, but that was only a come-on, a glowing preview of coming attractions. He wasn't a great player regardless of what the fawners and agents, talk show hosts and other jolly-up types told him. Not yet. It was pretty clear when he returned to Flushing to defend the title. He seemed relieved, almost glad, to lose to Jim Courier in the quarter-finals, to shed that hitch-hiker on his shoulders: the gorilla called 'Expectations'. It had been a lot to live up to, and he hadn't. His surrender was greeted cuttingly by former champion Jimmy Connors, who derided Pete for folding under pressure at the top, saying the greats, certainly himself, welcomed proving themselves again and again.

The jibes and the loss hurt, all right, but Pete was too young to handle it well. However, sheepish Pete had gone astray but momentarily. For one thing, Sam and Georgia Sampras didn't raise their boy to go big-time. His feet found the ground again, and he found a good shepherd to point him along the proper path on the proving ground: Tim Gullikson. "Tim changed my attitude. He helped me grow up," Pete would say of the excellent tutor/best friend whose loss he will mourn as long as he lives.

Counselling Pete, showing him how to connect all the talents of toughness and touch, as though blending a brass band with a chamber orchestra, Tim was along for the wonderful ride of three Wimbledons, two more US Opens and an Australian title. When Tim died Pete owned seven major singles titles, standing tall among American male paragons: Bill Tilden (10), Jimmy Connors (8), John McEnroe (7), Don Budge (6). He was younger at rolling seven than Tilden, Connors and McEnroe had been.

Not just 'could be' great by this time.

Naturally there will be setbacks, like losing his Wimbledon crown to Richard Krajicek in the fourth round, 1996. His neighbourhood is too spiky for him to bully all the inhabitants all the time. Still, they know who the boss is.

Perhaps his finest hour got the least attention. Pete was way out of his neighbourhood in November of 1995, tramping on muddy-looking clay within a deteriorating Moscow building called the

Olympic Stadium. It was a scene constructed specifically for Sampras — to trap him. A turgid dirt rectangle surrounded by a Russian chorus of 16,000 had been prepared for the Davis Cup finale, a hothouse retreat to three days of the old Cold War atmosphere.

No pulp fiction author could have outdone the wind-up of the world team championship in a cauldron of pressure that makes all other tennis events seem tepid. Not even a Wimbledon final is as emotionally demanding. Pete hadn't been a sensation in Davis Cup before this showdown occurring only blocks from the Kremlin, but he painted the town an unhappy red by scoring an amazing triple in the 3-2 US triumph.

"Anything it takes," he'd promised the US captain, Tom Gullikson [Tim's twin] in making the unexpected journey to Russia. Andre Agassi and Jim Courier were to handle the singles, while Pete accepted an invitation to play doubles only, something of a selfless comedown for the world No.1. But it was dreaded clay on which Andre and Jim figured to be surer. However, Agassi got hurt.

That meant it was Pete for the singles. For openers: a five-set drama with dirt-kicking desperado Andrei Chesnokov that hinged on one stroke — the last. In a frantic 23-stroke rally Pete knocked a ball that Chesnokov barely reached but couldn't quite coax into the US court. As he raised his arms in victorious relief at the 3-6, 6-4, 6-3, 6-7 (5-7), 6-4 outcome, Pete abruptly felt the world go upside-down. He was biting the dust, collapsing, and had to be lugged to the dressing-room, cramped, dehydrated. He had given everything — was anything left?

"If Chesnokov had kept the last point going I probably couldn't have played another," Pete shook his head. "If I get that ball I win by default," the Russian was bummed. But then Courier was beaten by the Russian ace, Yevgeny Kafelnikov. It was wobbly 1-1; the doubles became all important.

"I needed Pete," says Gullikson, "but it was up to him. Could he come back the next day, play all three days. Was he physically able? Would he be taking a chance playing doubles and screw up his singles the last day? Lucky for us, he wanted to. And did."

Oh, how he did. Clicking stupendously with Todd Martin, Pete was the right court cog in a go-ahead 7-5, 6-4, 6-3, stunning of Kafelnikov and Andrei Olhovskiy.

Day Three dawned, and there was Pete again, the essential element, the masterful and masterly performer in a 6-2, 6-4, 7-6 (7-4) victory over Kafelnikov. Launching 16 aces plus five service winners, and drilling 19 of those sweet swinging forehands on the run for winners — shots that made witnesses gasp with grudging admiration — Pete took Moscow in a manner that Napoleon and Hitler would have envied. Only nine predecessors in nearly a century of Davis Cup had registered such a triple to win the revered sterling crock.

All that on the treacherous terrain, the dreaded clay. The want-it-need-it hunger-talent glowed like one of the red stars atop the Kremlin. Keats would have called it poetic justice.

Bud Collins
August 1996

Part 1
US Open

Full Circle 1

ANDRE Agassi athletic? You can almost hear Pete Sampras saying, "Yeah, right." The Agassi across the net from Sampras, as they warmed up for the 1995 US Open final, may have been in the best shape of his life, may have been playing the best tennis of his life. But as usual with Agassi, he had been working an illusion, an image, all the while, even while working his way past Sampras to the No.1 world ranking.

It's to his credit he was able to do both.

Starved to perfection, stoked by new coach Brad Gilbert stroking the ball from the backcourt like none before him, Agassi seemed awesome, striding on to the National Tennis Center's stadium court.

But something was missing, as it always has been.

A wondrous tennis player, Agassi can at times be exposed as an average athlete.

Pete Sampras, to his credit, knew this, as he always has.

And so, five years after humbling Agassi in another US Open final he was not expected to win, Pete repeated the feat, although in much different fashion. In 1990 at the age of 19, he had simply steamrollered Agassi, winning in straight sets and dropping only nine games. This time he produced a thoughtful four-set victory, made possible by what Agassi couldn't do, as much as by what Sampras could.

It was a beautiful thing.

Pre-match counsel with on-site, ersatz coach Paul Annacone, mixed with guidance from true coach Tim Gullikson — offering what he could, via phone calls, while continuing his fight against brain cancer — yielded a clear consensus: the aim would be athletic, all-court points. The triumvirate reckoned, rightly as it turned out, that Andre would have no chance if versatility and adaptability came into play.

"Tim said that when Andre is in his comfort zone he'll beat most guys, and that I needed to try to do things to take him out of his zone," Sampras said months later, reflecting on his seventh Grand Slam title that brought him one step closer to Emerson, Laver, Rosewall and the accompanying immortality he craves, although downplays publicly.

"Whenever Andre and I play, I always feel like the first one who takes the initiative is who wins the point," Sampras added. "But Andre struggles a little bit when he's being moved around. That's what I tried to do."

And even though Sampras' scheme showcased his strengths — serving and volleying — while capitalising on Agassi's relative all-court weakness, one point that went against those grains is remembered most.

First set, set point. A 22-stroke backcourt rally that had Agassi written all over it. Sampras erased several potential winners, finally ending it with a crosscourt backhand winner.

"That point sucked... that point really sucked," Agassi said later, in a post-match interview in which he offered the lamest of excuses, saying he felt flat. Now *that* sucked.

Flat? For a Grand Slam final?

Talk about an illusion.

Sampras had his own, decidedly different magic act going five years earlier. He came into the 1990 Open seeded 12th. Earlier in the year he came out of nowhere, a gangly, stoop-shouldered kid with a huge serve, fluid style and quiet demeanour. A blend of cunning and casual, Sampras had emerged from a California junior career stunted by his switch from two hands to one on the backhand side, a change accompanied by new emphasis on covering the net. The changes had been urged by his first coach, Pete Fischer, who first moulded Sampras' game, then moulded his appreciation for the former greats, Aussies mainly, and their Grand Slam achievements.

The US Open was the first Grand Slam tournament Sampras played as a professional, in 1988, a first-round loss being a dubious highlight to a rookie year in which Sampras ended No.97 in the world rankings.

He got a wild-card berth into his first Open, his fourth wild card of the year, a perk that some argue made Sampras' initiation on to the tour far less of a hassle, in effect paving the way for his rise without the week-in, week-out concern of the odd upset.

There's some validity in that argument. But it's also worth noting that Sampras did pay some dues during his debut season.

He played — and survived — qualifying-draws in his first three events: Philadelphia, Indian Wells and the now-defunct Tournament of Champions in New York City; he won two of his five main-draw matches.

He slummed for a week, getting his first wild card at a USTA Challenger stop in Raleigh, North Carolina. Challengers are to the world tour what Triple-A baseball is to the major leagues. Sampras lost in the second round. If his sport were baseball, he might have been sent down to Double-A on the spot. In British soccer terms we could compare it to the difference between the FA Premiership and the Nationwide League.

Another wild card, this time to a world tour event in Schenectady, New York, paid off with his first real success making the semi-finals. He lost to Tim Mayotte, who labelled him as a 'player to watch'.

Schenectady boosted Sampras' ranking, earning him his first main-draw acceptance — and a No.3 seeding — at the Challenger in Seattle. Alas, another first-round loss. The next week, another Challenger and a fourth first-round defeat. No.5 then came at the

ATP Championships in Cincinnati — Sampras in via a wild card — at the sage hands of Brad Gilbert. That prefaced the early exit at the US Open.

By 1990, the argument against special treatment for the young gun was moot. Wild cards were no longer needed.

Sampras had started 1990 ranked 81st. He won his first professional tournament six months before the Open, beating Andres Gomez at the US Indoors. He took the Wimbledon warm-up on Manchester grass in June, but lost his first-rounder at Wimbledon itself.

Then came September, Flushing Meadow and lightning in a bottle in the form of seeing-eye serves travelling at 125mph, forceful first volleys, groundstrokes capable of breaking down any opponent, including the first inkling of what would eventually become a trademark shot, a running forehand that turned trouble into triumph, time after time.

Ivan Lendl fell in the quarter-finals, his string of nine consecutive US Open finals finished. Four-time champion John McEnroe's last stand ended in a four-set semi-final. Having defeated two men who had won seven US Open championships between them, Sampras took aim at Agassi, 20 years old, ranked No.4 in the world but considered an under-achiever after losing that year's French Open final to an already over-the-hill Gomez. Agassi, by most accounts, choked against Gomez.

By all accounts, there was no way to blame him this time around. The final was all over in one hour, 42 minutes, Sampras' serving — 13 aces, 12 service winners — the obvious key.

"I was serving so well, it put a seed in the other guys' minds: 'Play one bad game and the set could be over'," Sampras said. "It was the best I could possibly play, and it couldn't have been at a better time. I controlled the match and dictated play. I don't know if anybody could have beaten me."

Certainly not the over-matched Agassi. Image was worth nothing.

"When you can hit a serve 120mph on the line, there's not a lot you can do," said Agassi. "This was just an old-fashioned street mugging."

Old-fashioned indeed.

In playing the serve-and-volley style of old, albeit juiced by a Wilson Pro Staff now made of graphite instead of McEnroe's wood — and supplemented by an ability to stay back with the best of them, even Agassi and his retro-groundies — Sampras also unveiled another element to his throwback style.

Quiet off the court, he was even quieter on it. He would go about this with grace, we learned that September. As it used to be done, representing a clean break from the lineage of All-American rear-ends. (Connors begat McEnroe, who begat countless tennis brats across the land.) Sampras had no time for histrionics.

Because he was chasing history, and it was Lap 1.

"This is the ultimate in tennis," Sampras said after becoming the lowest seed to win the Open since a non-seed, Fred Stolle, in 1966.

He also had become the youngest men's champion, at 19 years and 28 days supplanting the 1890 title holder, Oliver S. Campbell — weak serve, decent slice, strong knickers, the legend goes — by five months.

"Nothing gets bigger than this; whatever I do the rest of my career I'll always be remembered as the US Open champion," Sampras said.

In retrospect, quite naive. Seven years later, Sampras already is seen as much more. And so much more is ahead. The legend, it seems, is in the works. But no matter how large it grows, it will forever be connected to that first US Open title.

"I don't think a lot about 1990," Sampras said before practising at his training headquarters in Wesley Chapel, Florida, 20 miles north of his home in Tampa. "But when I get to the Open each year and kind of walk the grounds I start thinking that 'hey, this is where my life changed.'

"You know, in 1990 I just kind of came out of nowhere."

And just as quickly, for a while, it seemed as if he might return.

Champp or Chump? 2

AS SOON AS the words were out of his mouth, Sampras wanted them back. He had just made the most untimely unforced error of the afternoon, far more grievous than any he committed in a 6-2, 7-6, 7-6 loss to Jim Courier, in the 1991 US Open quarter-finals.

"I'm kind of relieved," Sampras said, looking, sounding like a big, sorrowful wimp.

Uh-oh.

No less than Jimmy Connors jumped on that sentence and Sampras' contention that the pressure of being champion had made being champion a pain.

"That is the biggest crock I've ever heard, being relieved," said a once-again cocksure Connors, fresh from reaching the Open semis at the age of 39. "I spent my whole life trying to win seven [Opens] in a row, or whatever possible.

"To be the US Open champion is the greatest feeling you could have. And to try to do it again is what you live for. If these guys [now on tour] aren't living for that, something is wrong."

Courier couldn't believe it either.

"Really, how much pressure does Pete have?" Courier asked.

"He'll never have to work another day in his life. He's got millions in the bank and he's 20 years old. I really think he should be able to swing freely and have fun with the game. Everybody would trade places with him. He has the world at his feet.

"You should enjoy yourself in that situation. But each person is different in how they handle pressure."

Sampras had failed miserably in that regard.

After winning the Open in 1990, he finished the year with six victories and four defeats, then started slowly in 1991. As late as July, his record was only 16 wins and 11 losses.

"Maybe now I can go back to my normal lifestyle," Sampras said after losing to Courier. "The monkey is off my back. Maybe it can all go back to the way it was."

Honest stuff, there. Palatable, too.

But *relieved?*

"That really didn't come out right," Sampras said later. "The perception was that I was glad I lost. I wasn't relieved I lost, but I said it and everybody was on my butt about it."

Distaste for Sampras' post-match words was set up by the dismay at his on-court performance against Courier. Remember the serve that had severed Agassi? Sampras apparently couldn't. In the first set Sampras was broken twice via double-faults. Perhaps most telling was that Courier out-aced him.

"I've got a lot of tennis left in me," Sampras said during one of the few positive moments in the cathartic post-match interview.

Coming into the 1992 Open, Sampras had shown just that, winning pre-Open summer hard-court warm-up tournaments in Cincinnati (defeating Lendl) and Indianapolis (over Courier). Prior to those, he had even gone to Austria and beat Alberto Mancini in a clay-court final.

He was erasing the summer of 1991, altering his image as a sullen, sulking young man uncomfortable with his talent and unworthy of the praise accorded him initially.

He would finish the year 70-18, his first 70-victory season, with more than $1 million in earnings, and help the US win the Davis

Cup — after gagging badly the winter before, in Lyon, as France upset the Americans.

He had a new coach and sincere friend in Tim Gullikson. His first-ever, honest-to-goodness girlfriend in Delaina Mulcahy. Obviously, winning his first US Open may have changed Sampras' life, but not as much as his first date with Delaina. At Sampras' invitation, they took off for a week-long stay at a resort.

With his personal life going well, Sampras returned to New York in 1992 confident of his chances, seeded fourth. He needed confidence, to pull through some of the tough matches leading to a final against Stefan Edberg.

In the third round, always-dangerous Todd Martin extended Sampras to five sets. Afterward, Sampras said he probably would have gone down in 1991 faced with similar peril.

In the fourth round, Sampras needed five more to dismiss flashy Frenchman Guy Forget. In lieu of victory, Forget philosophised, regarding Sampras' tournament tightrope act.

"If you play with a crystal vase and throw it in the air, one day it is going to break," Forget cautioned. It was his roundabout way of labelling Sampras as fragile.

Sampras needed to beat Forget. He hadn't in the 1991 Davis Cup; Forget's four-set victory clinched France's upset. "I had to find a way to win," Sampras said.

It was a match that previewed a new aspect to Sampras' development as a player, as a champion. Playing at less than his best, he nonetheless pulled through.

Afterward, he admitted that such resolve had been in short supply in 1991. "I'm a lot more motivated," Sampras said. "I'm not sure I'm going to win the tournament; I'm not playing that great right now, but I'm fighting and winning. That's important to me."

Fighting. Winning. Calling it important. This was not a new Sampras, but a renewed Sampras. There would be no question of his effort or resolve this time. Thus, when it was obvious, in a quarter-final scolding of Alexander Volkov, 6-4, 6-1, 6-0, that his opponent had given less than his best, Sampras slid comfortably into a criticising mode.

Volkov had, of course, mailed it in, with this P.S.:

"Tanks a lot."

"He packed it in a little bit," Sampras said. "A match like this? A big opportunity? I was surprised, but I'll take it."

A rematch with Courier, then ranked No.1, would be quite different. Sampras won in four sets but paid for it significantly. Dehydration. Cramps. At least in the other semi, Edberg took five hours and 26 minutes to eliminate Michael Chang.

As Super Saturday segued into the tournament's second Sunday, it seemed like a wash.

No matter how significant the 1992 final was to Sampras, it was even more significant for the men's game as a whole. Once again, hindsight is working overtime, to provide that assessment.

Who could have predicted at the time that Edberg would soon fade from the upper echelon? Who could have foreseen Sampras' premature development into one of the game's all-time greats? And surely, no one could have imagined this would be their only Grand Slam title meeting, their only meeting in a final. No, the 1992 US Open final was simply another blue-chip event, with little significance attached to it past that moment.

Edberg planned to retire at the end of 1996; tennis fans should mourn the fact that he and Sampras didn't meet regularly in major finals. Separated by five years, they always have been joined by their sportsmanship and style. Beautiful people, playing beautiful tennis, both aspects coming naturally.

An unappreciated rivalry, perhaps, especially when cast against the glare of the Sampras-Agassi marketing machine. Sampras-Edberg stands as tennis' Ali-Norton, blown away by other matches, but resplendent in its own right.

Back to the moment. Sampras' mission was twofold: take the title and take back his words of 1991 via deeds of 1992. But mere survival had become a footnote, too. The wear and tear of making the final, especially the Open's inherent Super Saturday-final

Sunday grind, had taken a lot out of his 21-year-old body. The Courier match was an inkling: Sampras, despite his solid conditioning and athleticism, could be vulnerable if pushed too far physically; this was a criticism dating back to his junior days, when he was considered lazy, without motivation when it came to training.

Edberg? The defending champion had endured three consecutive five-setters. And of course, five sets against Chang is like seven or eight against anyone else.

"I'm fighting for my life out there," Edberg said. "I've been in a lot of trouble, but I think it proves I have good character and a lot of heart."

Character. That's what Sampras was really chasing, wasn't it? Or rather, the *image* of having character. He'd blown that image to hell and back the year before. What better time to repair, and gain respect, than in another final, against the consummate professional, the heir to Swedish supremacy, a man who had more than matched the standards of Bjorn Borg.

Both players advanced to the final on the strength of their serve, more than any other shot. Fittingly, it would be a breakdown of serve that decided things.

After a split of the first two sets, Sampras served for the third. He double-faulted twice, the second time on break point. Minutes later, in the tie-breaker, Sampras double-faulted at 4-5, handing the Swede two set points, and in effect, the match which Edberg went on to win 3-6, 6-4, 7-6 (7-5), 6-2.

"By the fourth set I was out of gas," Sampras said. "I was tired and exhausted. Mental exhaustion, more than anything. My serve kind of let me down."

Neither player put much stock in the No.1 ranking that accompanied this title — Sampras dropped to No.3, with Courier in the middle — preferring to emphasise instead the significance of a major championship.

And guess what? That significance was clear to Sampras, finally. In defeat, he sounded like a champion.

"At first, I didn't realise the history and importance of this tournament," Sampras said, misquoting his brain. He knew the history. He had a firm grasp of the importance. He just didn't appreciate it.

It had taken 1991's public ridicule for his flippancy, and losing in the 1992 final to make him see that.

"[Winning in 1992] would have meant more than 1990," Sampras said.

"Back then it all happened too fast."

Redemption 3

CEDRIC Pioline

Talk about a name made for tennis trivia.

It's a name Sampras would probably like to forget, even though Pioline was easy, straight-set pickings in the 1993 US Open final.

Therein lies the rub.

By reaching the final, Pioline became the story of the tournament. His loss to Sampras mattered not. He had already over-achieved, beating Courier in the fourth round and Wally Masur in the semis, to become the first Frenchman in 61 years to make the final.

Meanwhile, on the other half of the draw, Sampras progressed as expected — a four-set struggle with childhood foe Michael Chang the only semi-stumbling block — to follow up his first Wimbledon title with a run at his second US Open title, his third US Open final, his first on both Open counts as the world's No.1-ranked player.

Sampras' summer of 1993 was splendid, his Open fortnight the capper. He most certainly was worthy of a Courier, an Agassi, an Edberg, even on championship Sunday.

Instead he got a Pioline.

French toast. A low-ranking, non-seeded, backhand-slicing, no-tournament-winning Borotra/Lacoste wannabe who was in his first — and surely his last — Grand Slam final.

A major final with meagre mass appeal. Just great and bitterly ironic for Sampras, who was in the second half of a superb season, geared to reclaim the title he had won, then threw away, then yearned for, only to fall to two-time champion Edberg the year before.

Even if we didn't know Cedric Pioline, we knew he was no Stefan Edberg. A thinner, better-looking, right-handed Henri Leconte at best. Pioline's presence in the final would dilute the moment, Sampras' moment. No doubt about that. This had dud plastered all over it, destined to take its place alongside other momentous Grand Slam let-downs like McEnroe-Chris Lewis, Wimbledon 1983; Martina Navratilova-Zina Garrison, Wimbledon 1990.

But hey, it could have been worse.

Wally Masur could have made the final.

Typically, when a prospective final in a major championship doesn't pan out, it has been preceded by something momentous, somewhere in the draw, that ends up having a direct effect on the last day's proceedings. Garrison was an easy mark for Navratilova's ninth Wimbledon singles crown, but prior to that she upset Monica Seles and Steffi Graf in successive matches. Lewis got blown out by McEnroe, but in the semis had outlasted cannon-server Kevin Curren, who had upset Connors in the round of 16.

Likewise, the 1993 Open had its showcase, buried in a backlogged mid-week, rain-delayed schedule.

Call it boys to men.

On a late Wednesday night, Sampras and Chang renewed their rivalry that had started in 1980, near San Diego, in a boys 10-and-under tournament.

Southern California journalist Mark Winters remembers the rivalry as 'extraordinary', even during the juniors. But Winters adds that Sampras-Chang wasn't really what you'd call a rivalry back then since for both players, junior tennis was merely a means to a much grander end.

"Both those guys played up [in age classification]; they were building games, not rankings," Winters said. "Michael Chang was already Michael Chang. You had to beat him. Pete was a shotmaker who needed a little whiteout at times. Pete was a kid making *talent* mistakes."

Chang is the perfect source to describe Sampras' evolution. He remembers a different player, but one whose attitude was "pretty much the same as it is now; you know, very calm, very relaxed. But you wouldn't have recognised Pete. He just kind of got his serve in [without a lot of power] and didn't come in at all."

"Michael's been a great player as long as I've known him, when we were both eight years old," Sampras said.

Coming into the 1993 US Open quarter-final, Chang had won six of their eight matches on the pro tour, his grinding style having ground down Sampras more often than not. Each was secure in his simple but disparate approach. Sampras' power versus Chang's steadiness. That's what it was about. That's what it always will be about when these two play.

Fans who endured that day's eight-hour delay got two matches, really, in Sampras-Chang. Sampras snatched the match away from his lifelong pain-in-the-ass to play — Sampras has stuck that label to quirky Karsten Braach, but it adheres just as well to Chang — with a masterful last two sets, the sort of tennis that causes people to forget Tilden, McEnroe, Laver even.

Sampras periodically plays like that. Whenever Chang has been victimised, he immediately acknowledges what has taken place. Chang off-court isn't unlike his on-court self. He's a verbal backboard. Nothing fancy. Just the facts. Fundamentally sound responses. His demeanour always — *always* — is of Sampras-like proportions.

Even if his tennis is not.

So many times, victims of an 'in-the-zone' Sampras are asked what they could have done to stop the bleeding. So many times, the bull flows, as players try to convince questioners — and themselves, perhaps? — that they could have had a chance, had they just been alert to an adjustment here and there.

Once, after a particularly brutal beating, Chang was asked to pinpoint a Sampras weakness. "He doesn't cook very well," Chang answered, reminiscing painfully about some teenage angst in the form of some Sampras-prepared pasta.

Great stuff.

After this match — won 6-7, 7-6, 6-1, 6-1 by Sampras came this from Chang: "What could I do? I don't know... maybe go over and snap his strings? There's really nothing you can do. When he's playing his best he's practically unbeatable."

Practically unbeatable against Chang, certainly unbeatable against Pioline. Sampras dropped 11 games, regaining the world No.1 spot from Courier, becoming the first American since McEnroe in 1984 to sweep Wimbledon and the US Open.

Delaina said they'd both been on a natural high since Wimbledon. Now the sky was the limit. That first Open title that took Sampras to the top was in the distance — but it was not forgotten.

"In 1990 I was immediately recognised all over the world," Sampras said. "People were all over me, and I don't like being the centre of attention. It was from one extreme to the other, and for about six or eight months afterward I struggled with my life on and off the court. It was kind of a mess."

With this one in the books, Gullikson was starting to look like a better coach than he ever was a player. Sampras ended 1993 as the world's top-ranked player, finally rid of the inconsistency that had periodically plagued him in prime-time matches.

"Pete has a real hunger to stay at the top," Gullikson said.

What better place to dine than the US Open?

Sampras–Chang: Head To Head

The Pete Sampras-Michael Chang rivalry prefaced both players' pro careers, beginning at the 10-and-under level in California where Chang generally had the edge. As Sampras has risen in the pro ranks, he has finally started mastering Chang's game.

Sampras-Chang
1989–September 1996: Sampras 11, Chang 7

Tournament	Surface	Winner	Score
1989 Volvo International	Hard	Chang	6-4, 6-4
1989 Volvo Los Angeles	Hard	Chang	7-6, 6-0
1989 French Open	Clay	Chang	6-1, 6-1, 6-1
1990 Canadian Open	Hard	Chang	3-6, 7-6, 7-5
1990 ATP Championships	Hard	Chang	7-5, 6-4
1990 Grand Slam Cup	Carpet	Sampras	6-3, 6-4, 6-4
1991 Paris Indoor	Carpet	Sampras	2-6, 6-4, 6-3
1992 Lipton International	Hard	Chang	6-4, 7-6
1993 Grand Slam Cup	Carpet	Sampras	7-6, 6-3
1993 US Open	Hard	Sampras	6-7, 7-6, 6-1, 6-1
1994 Japan Open	Hard	Sampras	6-4, 6-2
1994 Wimbledon	Grass	Sampras	6-4, 6-1, 6-3
1994 Grand Slam Cup	Carpet	Sampras	6-4, 6-3
1995 Australian Open	Hard	Sampras	6-7, 6-3, 6-4, 6-4
1995 ATP Tour Finals	Carpet	Chang	6-4, 6-4
1996 Kroger/St Jude International	Hard	Sampras	6-3, 6-2
1996 Salem Open	Hard	Sampras	6-4, 3-6, 6-4
1996 US Open	Hard	Sampras	6-1, 6-4, 7-6 (7-3)

The Agony And The Agassi 4

SAMPRAS had — and still has — a history of being prone to illness, injury or late-match exhaustion, a puzzling problem for an athlete of his stature who at times seems so rock-solid. But Gullikson, with the help of Tampa, Florida, fitness guru Pat Etcheberry, was working hard to rectify that in 1993 and 1994. In between tournaments, Sampras could be found running in the sugary-white sand of a beach volleyball court, strapped into a harness, with a barking, growling Etcheberry attached to the other end. As Sampras' shoes sank into the sand with each laboured step, he seemed to get ever closer to the fitness enjoyed by hard-body rivals like Courier, who also trained with Etcheberry, or Thomas Muster, a clay-court master mainly because of conditioning.

Shin splints and shoulder problems for Sampras at one time seemed almost chronic. By mid-1994 they had been minimised, at a time when Sampras' talent was being maximised. Sampras had won the Australian Open and Wimbledon titles, giving him three of the last four Grand Slams. He enjoyed a huge lead in the ATP Tour point standings.

A week after defeating Goran Ivanisevic in the Wimbledon final, Sampras was en route to The Netherlands, for a Davis Cup competition against the Dutch, on hard courts. Having gone from grinding and sliding on European clay to the slippery challenge of English grass, Sampras found the sudden pounding of a firmer surface too much to take. He left The Netherlands with a serious case of tendinitis in his left ankle.

There ensued what Sampras would call his 'lost summer'. On the cusp of autumn, he returned to the Open determined to defend but realistically just trying to survive. Hoping for the best, half-expecting the worst, which he got. It went by the name of Jaime Yzaga, a pleasant fellow from Peru who's a drag to play, if he's allowed to play *his* game, which consists of knocking a zillion balls back until the other guy gives up, either out of boredom, exasperation or exhaustion.

In 1994 Sampras withdrew from four consecutive tournaments between Wimbledon and the US Open, including the classic hard-court affairs in Cincinnati and Indianapolis, where the mid-summer Midwestern heat is hell, but prepares players for whatever Flushing Meadows can present. It's a brutal stretch, but necessary, at least in an abridged version.

Sampras stayed home in Tampa during that time. He rode an exercise bike to help make up for the lack of training, but his cardiovascular capacity was dropping daily. Then, just as his ankle was feeling better, the pain returned. An MRI, only two days before the Open began, showed a calcium deposit. Sampras received an anti-inflammatory injection. The next day he practised for two hours with Edberg and for 45 minutes with Gullikson.

The ankle stiffened.

So did his resolve.

''There's no instant cure for the ankle, or the missed time," he said. "And there's no reason to talk about it. You make the best of what you've got. It's time to play."

The tennis world, and whatever portion of the public who cared to notice, was on the precipice of learning much more about Pete Sampras than many thought possible. At a time when his tennis reputation was growing exponentially, so was the criticism that he was perhaps ruining pro tennis. There was a growing consensus that Sampras had a problem. He was too good. On and off the court. Oh, there were the odd rumours that he actually did have a personality. There was a saltiness to his speech, it was said. Ol' Pete wasn't always sweet. Catch him in the right setting and the four-letter words flew. He seemed to have a special penchant for the f-word. Had a knack for using it two or three times per sentence. A 'good' curser, Trumanesque. Word had gotten out around his adopted hometown of Tampa that he flashed occasional cheapskate tendencies. Weak tipper, were the whispers. He had a habit of under-dressing, showing up a bit too casual at times, when a sport coat would have been apropos. And then there was Delaina, an older woman, of all things. Shameful to some, inspirational to others.

But that, alas, was about it. Nothing of substance to get really upset, or in the least gossipy, about. The Delaina thing had potential but as that relationship endured there seemed little to talk about there, either.

Sampras' vanilla personality did not make for good copy. Neither did the way he rolled over opponents. Much of this backlash began at Wimbledon, when en route to the 1993 title he made grass seem an almost ludicrous surface for the modern game. The London tabloids accorded cursory consideration of his talent, apparent amnesia erasing memories of big hitters like Roscoe Tanner, Phil Dent or Kevin Curren, whose serving ruined many a potential grass-court rally.

Sampras became 'Sampraz..z..z' in the headlines. Of course, American journalists had done their own damage to his image early on, after the 1991 US Open.

But at least there seemed to be truth to that lashing.

Since then, Sampras had done nothing to indicate he was

anything but a great guy and greater champion. By and large, it wasn't enough. He needed a defining moment and up to that point sheer, simple excellence had not been enough to earn universal media approval.

Make what you will of that. Blame it on the 1990s. Blame it on Agassi and his image-is-everything persona. Or maybe on some of the big names in other sports, like the Chicago Bulls basketball star Dennis Rodman, a multi-coloured scapegoat, the antithesis of vanilla.

That said, three hours and 34 minutes of Jaime Yzaga, God bless him, was time well-spent on September 7, 1994.

Sampras without legs was still pretty tough. And as he slid through the first two rounds easily enough, he looked capable of playing his way into shape. Thing is, the US Open is not the NBA. Eighty-two basketball games gives one time to coast, cruise and eventually sprint all night. Seven tennis matches? Quite different. If you're not full-speed from the get-go, it is unlikely — virtually impossible — to step up at some point during the US Open, where the scheduling, the crowds, the hard courts and occasionally the heat wear you down perhaps more than any other event. Grass courts — that is probably the only surface where below-par fitness can be disguised via quick points. But in the glare of New York, you are naked, or at least partially exposed when forced to hit ball after ball when your body is not up to it.

Sampras' inevitable stutter-step came in the third round against an opponent just as pesky as Yzaga, but using a different style.

Roger Smith had beaten Sampras in their only previous match, a qualifying encounter in the late 1980s. Smith's game has the potential to puzzle anyone. He mixes sound tennis with the odd off-beat risk. He can chip-and-charge decently, or rally effectively. Serves pretty well, too. The variance made Sampras appear vulnerable for a while, but it was dismissed after Sampras' four-set victory as nothing more than a temporary fly in the ointment.

This match also underscored Sampras' new status. He was starting to be viewed as the second coming of Laver, wherein any sort of hiccup was considered momentous. No matter the opponent's talent. Sampras had reached a higher plane. If Roger Smith could take a set, then someone else surely could take two and, yes, perhaps three, because clearly Sampras wasn't right.

"I just felt a little sluggish," Sampras said, adding that the ankle felt fine, that he had been hoping to avoid such a struggle against such a no-name, but it couldn't be helped because "I didn't really have the preparation I was hoping for coming into the Open."

Yzaga also had a previous victory over Sampras, at the Open no less. In 1988, Sampras' first Open, Yzaga knocked him out in the first round, initiating a surprising scuffle of a rivalry. They had split four matches overall. Yzaga, a backcourt counter-puncher, seemed to match up well with Sampras for some reason. Hard to believe? Well, at various stages of his undistinguished but steady career, Yzaga has developed a knack for matching up well with just about anyone.

This time, Yzaga did more than that, much more, in extending Sampras to a fifth set, then taking a 5-2 lead. Sensing Sampras wasn't up to snuff at the outset, Yzaga started fast. Then, in the fifth, as he watched Sampras struggle for his wind between points, his confidence grew.

At that point fate stepped in. In that last 45 minutes, Sampras became even more a champion than before, in defeat.

So he lost. So what? If ever the rest of the men's tour had a reason to fear Sampras, it was that afternoon. Feet blistered, ankle aching, back cramping, mouth agape, he lasted until the 12th game of the final set. Yzaga had to caress a tricking backhand return crosscourt to close out. Sampras stumbled to the net, too tired to realise his accomplishment. After all, he had lost.

Tennis had won. Something special had taken place. It made sense, now, why Sampras lacked personality. He was too full of character.

The display continued after the match. Sampras didn't show for the post-match press conference. Word spread he might not show at all, that he was ill. Yzaga came in and spoke briefly, then fled himself, with stomach cramps.

Instead of Sampras, doctors were summoned by the USTA. They gave a long-winded, almost comical explanation of Sampras' condition. The docs droned on and on, responding to questions that fed on the answers, becoming increasingly technical. "What is this, the Kennedy assassination press conference?" whispered one journalist. "If this keeps up, I'm yelling out, 'was Governor Connally hit?'"

You had to listen closely. If you did, you heard the news. Sampras was worn out, dehydrated. That was all. That was everything.

He also was en route. No doubt prompted by Tim Gullikson, Sampras came in, sat down and politely offered no excuses, only reasons, why he was out of the tournament everybody expected him to win.

"Things kind of caught up with me and I didn't have anything left," Sampras said. "In the third set I felt my recovery between points taking longer and longer. Both feet are sore. The whole body is sore. I just felt like I'm not in great shape right now. I was probably in worse shape today than I've ever been in a match.

"It was, well, just my pride that kept me going. I figured that if he was going to beat me, I wanted him to go the distance. I wasn't even thinking about retiring. I wasn't going to retire and let him not earn it."

Yzaga also had earned a place in history. A footnote, sure, but it was something. Before rushing from his post-match talk, Yzaga already was talking reflective. It already had started to sink in.

"He never gave up, Yzaga said. "I congratulate him. Obviously he wasn't feeling well, but that's what makes him a champion. He kept fighting until the end."

Sampras didn't hang around New York. He missed Andre Agassi's run to the title, although he did more or less predict it before bolting.

He left running on empty, after admitting that for the latter part of the Yzaga match, he ran on adrenalin, responding to the crowd.

"I didn't have anything left," Sampras said. "It was nice to have everyone behind me."

Agassi. Sampras knew he was coming. At some point. He had to, Sampras figured. That figuring can be traced to the 1992 Davis Cup quarter-finals, when Agassi saved Sampras — and the United States — from embarrassment, winning two matches, including the clincher, in a 3-2 victory against Czechoslovakia.

The competition was played in Fort Myers, Florida, in March, hotter than hell. With a chance to clinch, Sampras wilted in the reverse singles, losing to Big-Bird lookalike Petr Korda. Agassi, having drummed Korda the first day, did the same to Karel Novacek. Sampras came away incredibly impressed, and he has used that weekend as a reference point in currently assessing what he always felt was Agassi's inevitable run at him, at the top of the rankings.

"I remember watching him play those matches and I said that if he played like that every week he could be No.1 in the world," Sampras told *Tennis* magazine.

"Sitting there [watching him play] I just couldn't understand why he couldn't do that week in and week out.

"He just played unbelievable tennis. Seeing him prepare during the week. Seeing him get ready for his matches, he seemed like he was really in focus and geared up to play."

Pro tennis was calling to Agassi that autumn of 1994. The women's game was in a shambles. Monica Seles, stabbed in 1993, had yet to return. Steffi Graf was battling a bad back. Jennifer Capriati had been arrested twice in the previous year, once for shoplifting, the second time on a marijuana possession charge.

Sports Illustrated's spring story entitled 'Is Tennis Dying?' had pointed out the game's other problems that certainly included the men's tour and its reputation for a rash of matches being 'tanked' or given away by unmotivated players.

And then there was Sampras, whose domination was overshadowing his ability.

For some, it hurt to acknowledge Agassi as a possible saviour, even after his stirring 1994 Open final victory over Michael Stich. Agassi was unseeded at that Open, the result of a late-1993 wrist injury and subsequent surgery that took him off the ATP Tour and out of the top 20. That was an anomaly, of course, quite clear when Agassi ran through the Open field that was missing Sampras the second week.

Professional tennis needed further help entering 1995. Solutions to the game's myriad of problems would be long-term, but Agassi-Sampras — with both players now at the top of their respective, disparate games — represented at least one quick fix. There had been an inkling of the rivalry's potential in the 1994 Lipton Championship final, in Key Biscayne, Florida. Sampras woke up with a serious stomach problem. The ailment soon was traced to a questionable room-service order of pasta and red sauce. Sampras came to the Crandon Park Tennis Center hoping to play the final, but as match time approached it was clear he wouldn't be able to go. Agassi offered to wait while he recovered. It was widely, overly lauded as a momentous act of sportsmanship. Agassi simply wanted to play, having fought through the draw to make his second final of the year. A match against Sampras, at the time far and away the world No.1, would be the consummate indicator of where his wrist, his game and his head were at the moment. He needed the match much more than Sampras did.

So he waited. Sampras got it together, then went out and slowly worked his way into the match, which he won in three sets. "If I can't beat Pete when he's sick I don't deserve to win the tournament," Agassi said.

They met three more times in 1994, Sampras winning twice, including a semi-final at the ATP Tour Championships. They went into 1995 with Sampras holding a 7-5 head-to-hair advantage.

At the Australian Open, the rivalry could rightfully be labelled head-to-head. Agassi had finally cut his shoulder-length hair during a champagne-laced evening at the New York apartment of his girlfriend, actress Brooke Shields. The effect was to make him appear even more radical than before. Agassi had gone from rock star to pirate. He took to wearing bandanas over his buzz-cut. His outfits, by Nike, were becoming more outlandish all the time.

Sampras was emerging as the perfect straight man, especially since he also was Nike-sponsored. His clothing was conservative, many times based in white and beige. His shoes looked pretty normal, too, while Agassi's appeared to be glorified hiking boots. Nike was in the process of cornering all aspects of the apparel market with these two individuals. There would be times in 1995 when the marketing scheme, so contrived yet so natural, playing off the personalities of the two, blurred the importance of the tennis.

The tennis, though, always came back. It was, after all, the foundation of this rivalry, again because of contrast. Sampras' serving. Agassi's returning. Sampras at the net, Agassi at the base-line. Sampras' fluid athleticism. Agassi's dogged, bludgeoning style.

Agassi's four-set victory over Sampras in the Australian final didn't get its due. Everybody was still talking about Sampras' quarter-final against Jim Courier. Tim Gullikson had flown back to the United States, diagnosed with brain cancer, to start an 18-month doomed battle for his life. As Sampras was struggling against Courier, a fan yelled for him to win it for Gullikson, and Sampras broke down, somehow continuing to hit shots through the tears.

Likewise, their second meeting of 1995 got short shrift, but blame that on Sampras. In the Indian Wells final, he hit some of the best groundstrokes in his life to win in straight sets. On to the Lipton, where a rematch, won by Agassi, bounced off a backdrop of mutual admiration. During the event, both announced they would immediately fly to Italy afterward and represent the US in a second-round Davis Cup competition. At this point, the rivalry was starting to be hyped as a relationship. The ATP Tour and Nike, and whatever tournaments the two appeared in, wanted everyone to believe these guys were buddies until the bell rang. Agassi slipped into this act easier. Sampras went along, even to the point of flying on Agassi's private jet after the Lipton final to New York. The players watched Shields perform on Broadway, in

Grease. They then went on to London via the Concorde, then to Palermo where they led the victory against the Italians.

Sampras didn't want to go to Palermo, at least not with Agassi. The contrasts that make their rivalry so real on court, make a relationship virtually impossible off court. Sampras says they never talk, unless they're at a tournament or doing a promotion. "Do we ever just pick up the phone, dial each other up and talk, just like that?" Sampras said. "Uh-uh. We don't."

Agassi has an entourage, with Shields at the point. A bodyguard. A chattering coach in Brad Gilbert. Someone to carry his bags. Sampras had Gullikson until he fell ill. Now it's quiet-guy Paul Annacone, a sharp guy but one whose chief task may be worrying about keeping the gut in Sampras' racquets. Todd Snyder, former ATP trainer in his second year of working for Sampras, is usually on the scene. Delaina Mulcahy tended to pick and choose her appearances. One more thing. Sampras carries his own bags. As for a bodyguard, get real.

With Agassi, life is a show. For Sampras, it's almost as if tennis is an intrusion into his existence.

"They're just very dissimilar people — but they can get along," says veteran tennis reporter Sandra Harwitt. The difference lies in the fact that "Pete is very self-assured. He doesn't need all the trappings, like Andre, to know he's successful."

When the tennis turned into a show in 1995, and it was certainly that, Sampras went along with it. The rivalry was making money, helping tennis and at times, sure, it was a lot of fun, even if Agassi's act was a bit much. The commercials they made in San Francisco and London were classics: hopping out of cars, stopping traffic, they put up a net in the middle of the streets and started rallying, right there. And besides, at times the friendship actually did seem real, if not deep. Sampras turned 24 during the ATP Championships in Cincinnati. Agassi found out it was his birthday and arranged for a cake and an impromptu party at the players' hotel. Sort of like the old days, when Laver, Newcombe and the boys used to knock a few back and chat about the day's play. It was another indication that Agassi wanted to make the friendship as legitimate as possible given the confines of competition.

"Certain aspects of this rivalry are quite refreshing," says Harwitt. "For instance, that they actually *can* have a rapport of some sort. Like at Cincinnati. Do they do that at every tournament? No. But maybe they get together a couple of times a year. You never saw John McEnroe and Jimmy Connors going out together. Pete and Andre can do that. They can socialise. I don't think there's any real dislike between them."

More evidence of that came when Agassi heard about comments by McEnroe that depicted friendship between top rivals as virtually impossible, that for rivalries to truly thrive, they must be round-the-clock.

"I think John is the kind of guy that likes a lot of tension in a lot of relationships in his life," Agassi said, right before the Open. "I'm just not quite sure he is easy with anything being easy.

"He never stayed in the same hotel as Connors and there is a downside to that, too. And it's unfortunate because I think it reflects poorly on what this game is all about."

Was that real or was it image-driven? Hard to tell with Agassi. But whatever, it read well, on the eve of the Open. And it bounced solidly off a concurrent report that stripped the rivalry — and Sampras — clean. *The New York Times* Sunday magazine left Sampras pondering one of the few truly negative profiles written about him. Not counting London, of course.

"I learned a lot about the media on that one," Sampras said several months later, shaking his head. "Some of the things written. calling me foul-mouthed, that sort of thing…"

Sampras claims that casual conversation made its way into print. If that's true, it's still not much of a defence.

What happened is Sampras got nailed, and he didn't like it.

Nailed for using the famous four-letter word, albeit, again, in hilarious style. For making light of Delaina's feelings — he jokingly cast her as a gold-digger. For acting cool and cocky, the antithesis of the Sampras most people know. For showing little regard for his interim coach, Annacone, when some tennis stratagems were tossed around.

The piece was brilliant in its bite. And it has affected Sampras noticeably. He's no longer profane at the drop of a hat around media, even those he trusts the most. A sort of damage control mentality now guides his syntax. He's gone from Truman to Reagan.

The timing of the piece was perfect, too. It added an enticing, exciting footnote to the rivalry, setting up a US Open final between the two in a fashion that was, somehow, both roundabout and presumptuous. Of course, journalists throughout the world were doing the same thing, perhaps just not as effectively. It was left to Sampras and Agassi to do their part.

Agassi, who displaced Sampras atop the world rankings in the spring, beat him just two weeks before the US Open, in the final at Montreal. It was a disappointing day; Sampras won the first set before dropping the next two, sucked into trading groundstrokes with Agassi. That started a mediocre post-Wimbledon run for Sampras, a pre-Open period that featured, after Montreal, a quarter-final loss to Michael Stich at Cincinnati, and a semi-final loss to Bernd Karbacher at Indianapolis. Two Germans getting some watered-down revenge for Boris Becker in America's heartland.

Agassi, meanwhile, had won everything since Wimbledon with only a minor stumble or two. For all his apparent flakiness, the guy buckles down to play his best on hellishly hot hard courts, generally thriving on conditions that can humble others.

The titles rolled in for Agassi, and even his staunchest critics had to stand back and take a second look. Agassi put together one of the best summers in the history of the tour, starting in Washington, D.C., where he was nearly overcome by the heat before finishing off Stefan Edberg. A final worth noting, indicative of Agassi's development as a competitor. He vomited several times during changeovers. It was exactly the sort of situation that would have spelled defeat earlier in his career.

Seven days later came the win over Sampras in Montreal. Agassi took a week off, then grabbed two more titles, beating Michael Chang at the ATP Championships in Cincinnati and Richard Krajicek at the Volvo International in New Haven, Connecticut.

Sampras, though, waved off Agassi's momentum prior to the Open. At first it sounded like a rare hint of bravado, as Sampras, sitting poolside at Saddlebrook Resort near his home in Tampa, likened Agassi's run to his own in 1992 when he won at Kitzbuhel, Cincinnati and Indianapolis. Reflecting on that summer, he recalled how success ended up costing him, how he peaked in the Midwest, of all places, instead of New York.

Not that Sampras spent much time worrying about Agassi. Sampras, by and large, worries about Sampras, a stance that goes back to Pete Fischer, who instilled in his pupil at a very young age a feeling that he should, and could, control his destiny whenever he stepped on to a tennis court. But Sampras also faced the reality of another destiny spinning out of control that he had not the slightest chance of altering. Gullikson's condition had worsened. Facing a new, intense round of chemotherapy, he cancelled plans to attend the 1995 Open.

At the same time, Sampras was buoyed by at least knowing he was better prepared than the year before, when his lack of conditioning caught up to him against Yzaga.

"I've played some more and I feel like I'm ready to go," he said, the weekend before the tournament began. "I am fit and ready to battle three out of five sets in the heat, whatever it's going to take at this point. Obviously Tim is not …he was hoping to come to one of the summer tournaments and the Open. That was kind of our plan.

"So compared [to 1994] I'm more prepared. I wasn't at my best physically. I felt like I was hobbling around."

When the Open men's draw was released, the hype was on. Anything less than Agassi-Sampras in the final, well, just wouldn't do. After both easily won first-round matches, both tried their best to downplay the urge to look ahead.

Agassi, always able to be more open than Sampras, even divulged that the hype was starting to get to him.

"I have to say that it's really difficult going into a tournament and everyone expecting you to play," Agassi said. "You have to truly force yourself not to think about it. You're trying to convince everybody that Pete is not on your mind. You're trying to convince yourself of the same thing because you know there are other guys who can beat you."

"Everyone's assuming that [we'll play in the final], expecting that, but that's the last thing on my mind," Sampras said. "It would be great to get to the final and play anyone, but there's a lot of time ahead. This isn't like Martina and Chris used to be [on the women's professional tour]. Everybody knew they'd get to the final each week. That's not going to happen in the men's game."

Just talk? Maybe not. Maybe Sampras really was taking things one match at a time, since next up was none other than Yzaga, who had to know he would have a much different fight on his hands than the year before.

Sampras and Yzaga go back a way at the US Open, long before 1994. Sampras, at the age of 17, drew Yzaga in the first round of his first Open. Into the main draw thanks to a wild-card berth, Sampras won the first two sets but lost the next three. The very next year they met in the third round, Sampras coming off a five-set victory over defending champion Mats Wilander, perhaps the first truly huge singles breakthrough of his pro career. (Earlier that year he and Jim Courier had won the Italian Open doubles.) Sampras dealt with Yzaga's steadiness this time, winning in four sets after dropping the first.

Yzaga had thus always played Sampras tough in New York, but always with extenuating circumstances, either the hindrance of youthful inexperience, the inevitable let-down post-Wilander or 1994's fatigue-ridden fall that Sampras was determined to erase, extinguish — pick your verb — in 1995.

And so he did, starting his first service game with a 130-mph missile. One game featured aces of 123, 127, 128, part of a 16-ace total overall. Not a particularly high number, simply because Sampras wasn't on court long enough. Erasure was a clean swipe, taking 92 minutes; 6-1, 6-4, 6-3, two sets and two hours less than the previous year's character-building ordeal.

"Once I saw the draw and the possibility of playing Jaime I was looking forward to it," Sampras said. "We were going to battle because what happened last year really didn't sit well with me. I was very disappointed at the time. I wasn't in shape for that match. I was unprepared. You know, you never forget a loss like that, especially at a major championship. I was ready to go from the first point on. I got off to a great start and that kind of set the tone for the match. This time the adrenalin was really kicking in. I was really pumped. It was just a matter of staying aggressive and not hitting any loose errors."

Aggression is Australian Mark Philippoussis' strong suit, which presented Sampras with a completely different challenge in the third round. Philippoussis, then 18 years old, has the look of an NFL linebacker at 6ft 4ins, 220 pounds. He also has the look of a Sampras, with the same bushy eyebrows, products of their Greek heritage. And he also has the serve of a Sampras, only a bit wilder and a good bit harder.

One can envision a Sampras-Philippoussis rivalry developing at some point, maybe after Sampras has started to age and fade, concurrent with Philippoussis coming of age. For now, the Australian man-child is threatening, no more, but certainly no less, as Sampras would find out four months later, at the Australian Open.

"He's the type of player you get absolutely no rhythm against," Sampras said after a four-set victory. "He's out there going for huge second serves. I had problems returning *both* his serves the whole match. When you look at someone that young, you look to see if he has a weapon. And he definitely has a weapon: his serve. But he's got a huge game [overall]. And he doesn't really play with a high level of percentages. But that's what makes him so dangerous."

Old foe/old friend Todd Martin didn't last long in the fourth round, Sampras aces keying a three-set win. A quarter-final against surprise opponent Byron Black also was through in straights, after

22 aces. That brought Sampras to the semis against Courier, who had looked quite like his former top-ranked self in beating Michael Chang.

Sampras and Courier no longer are automatically on opposite halves of the draw. Not since Courier's bulldog backcourt game started wavering a couple of years ago, and his world ranking fell accordingly. But Sampras knows the numbers mean little when the two play. "When I play Jim I don't feel like I'm playing someone No.15; I feel like I'm playing a top five player," Sampras says.

Whenever they play, they seem to almost mesh, each player copying what the other does better. Courier starts serving harder. Sampras stays back a bit more. Either way, rare is the rally where the ball isn't being crunched, repeatedly, with the occasional Sampras chip-charge-drop volley sequence one of the few moments of touch to be displayed.

The 1995 Open semis was their third Flushing Meadow match, with Sampras coming in with a 13-3 lifetime edge over Courier, one of the three losses in that dreadful, heartless 1991 quarter-final. That's an incredible numerical advantage, considering the many close matches they'd played. But Sampras, in his rise to the top of rankings, had started developing a true champion's habit of playing big points perfectly or close to it.

"When you play Jim it always comes down to a couple of points and I just happened to win the right point," Sampras said. "I thought the level of tennis was quite high. My game matches up pretty well with Jim. I'm just trying to keep the ball away from his forehand. That's the bottom line against Jim. You try to do that and hopefully get some errors off the backhand side. But when it comes down to the points I'm just trying to stay aggressive. I'm trying to produce a winner, because sometimes I get screwed when I'm in a defensive position."

Sampras needed four sets this time, four tough sets: 7-5, 4-6, 6-4, 7-5. But since they were played at the start of 'Super Saturday', he had an immediate advantage over Agassi, who beat Boris Becker that night in the other semi.

"The big points didn't go my way," Courier said, summing up both the match and the rivalry with Sampras. "And it's my responsibility to make them go my way. Pete's got a lot of confidence in himself to go for the big shots at the big times. When that works out you look like a genius. When it doesn't work out you don't look so great.

"For him, it's been working out most of the time."

The second men's semi-final on Saturday at the Open is never the desired one. Invariably the winner is off the court in early evening, with the prospect of a late afternoon final the next day. But that's 'Super Saturday', the Open's annual made-for-television orgy that has been modified, starting last year; the women's final, previously held between the men's semis, was moved to the tournament's last Sunday, joining the men's final.

Agassi was tired and angry after finishing off Becker, not ideal moods considering what was ahead. The handshake after the match lasted a split second, maybe less. Becker had blasted Nike, Agassi's sponsor, after Wimbledon, in print. Becker also had targeted Agassi.

"It was a two-page article that yielded so many comments about other players not liking me, me not hanging out in the locker room, me not practising with the other guys," Agassi said. "I couldn't understand it. I go to sleep at night feeling like I am respected and liked."

Agassi is indeed respected and liked, downright popular with most other players despite his rock-tour style of going about his tennis. But Becker shrugged off Agassi's comments, standing by his right, as an elder statesman of the tour, to bitch and moan. At least he offered a slightly conciliatory tone. As for the final, Becker wisecracked, "it's the match everyone wants to see, isn't it?"

Agassi didn't need additional confrontation. But he did need some rest. It indeed had been a long summer; since losing to Becker in the Wimbledon semis, Agassi had won 26 consecutive matches.

"Andre has less time to regroup and less time to get ready for [the final] but you know, he has done it before," Becker said. "It is a US Open final. I think he can get up one more day to play great tennis. It should be a very exciting match to watch, even for me."

The US Open is tennis at its most gladiatorial.

The spectators are an amalgam of the knowledgeable and ignorant, the drunk and sober, the crude, rude and reserved. But almost all are generally hot and bothered by the time the tournament's second Sunday rolls around. The fact that the men's final is played in late afternoon, to maximise television exposure, heightens the mood.

This is the major tournament where decorum is checked at the door, where it's not uncommon for a heckler to wait until a server is just about to strike a crucial second ball, then yell as loudly as possible. It's a crowd that has no problems siding with a particular player, whether it's based on popularity, or, as often happens, on effort. They want to see some blood spilled. That's what made Connors so popular there and, to a slightly lesser extent, McEnroe. That's why stoicism, personified by players like Bjorn Borg or Ivan Lendl, always received restrained praise.

"The crowd is very loud," says Sampras. "It's a constant buzz. Everyone is moving around. You're playing tennis but they're not really watching the match. It's like they're all talking. That's the first thing I noticed the first time I stepped on the stadium court. It's such a big stadium. The crowd is kind of into it. But it's a strange crowd versus, say, a Wimbledon crowd."

But when they *do* get into it, Sampras added, "you can't get more exciting fans than in New York. It has its own unique personality just like all the majors do. It's just different. As far as the majors it's a little bit inconvenient. When I walk on to the grounds, it's a pretty long walk to the practice courts and the stadium and you're basically out in the public a lot of the time. I don't mind signing autographs, but there are times when you want to be alone and go to your practice court and not be bothered.

"But, you know, it *is* the US Open. You just have to deal with it and understand this is what makes it unique in a lot of ways."

In terms of romance with the Open crowds, Agassi falls into the Connors-McEnroe category because of his flamboyance, the way he shares every emotion with the fans. Sampras' style would seem to relegate him to the second, stoic group, but he has risen above that by the sheer brilliance of his game.

Sampras and Agassi: warriors in the arena that for all the everyday people, featured the beautiful ones, too. After the match Sampras joked about hitting an ace and looking up into the stands to see John F. Kennedy Jr. "Honest to God," Sampras said. "I thought, 'Hey, he looks pretty familiar'."

Another moment early on, Sampras noticed movement in the crowd behind him. No wonder. Arnold Schwarzenegger was finding his seat. "I looked over and there he was, 'The Terminator'," Sampras said.

Out of the blocks, the match developed into an early stand-off, very important for Agassi. The longer he stayed with Sampras, on serve, the better. There always was the chance that at some point, Sampras' attacking artistry would break down briefly, allowing Agassi an opening, especially considering the day's swirling wind that plagued ball tosses and at times actually favoured the man hitting *into* it. After the first nine games, they were on serve, Agassi having won his first 11 service points, a rare show of dominance from the line, especially against Sampras. With Agassi serving at 30-30, the match's first moment of sheer, dumb luck came Sampras' way, as a forehand rode the net, then trickled down, for a winner.

A first set point slipped away, as a safely played Sampras service return fluttered into mid-net. At deuce, Agassi blasted a high forehand volley long. A mile long. A first sign of nervousness? Not really. It was the first vivid example of Agassi's vulnerability when forced to come off the baseline and try to 'feel' a shot instead of blast one.

"The ball was moving around [in the wind]," Agassi said. "It was kind of a bit awkward for me. It started moving and I just second-guessed it a little bit. I think I was also giving some respect to his running forehand. He likes to cover the shot and hit it big, so I just missed it [crosscourt]. I made an error there, and that was it."

That gave Sampras a second set point, the one played out over 22 strokes, a point — it shall forever be known as *The Point* — that Nike would base another Sampras-Agassi commercial on the next year.

How good a point? It left no less than John McEnroe blubbering, "the power, the angle, the depth, the importance — wow." McEnroe went so far as to say it was the best baseline point he'd ever seen.

"It was probably one of the best points I have ever been a part of," Sampras said. "If I'd lost it I would have felt a lot worse, that's for sure. We were both running each other around and I just flicked off a good backhand. I was pretty winded after that, but I regained my composure and played a pretty good first game [to hold serve starting the second set]. That was a huge point. It was unbelievable. Thank God I won it."

Did that one rally, that one point, decide the match? Hard to say. It certainly was a microcosm of Sampras' superiority on this day and in some ways, the rivalry as a whole.

For someone watching their first Sampras-Agassi, it was a study guide.

"I'm not going to say that one point didn't make a difference," Agassi said. "I mean, it got him the first set. But I ended up getting back into it.

"Even though I ran Pete 12 corners that point, he wanted it and he knew it was going to have a big impact on his confidence. He worked hard for it and got it. I think that's what makes Pete such a great player — his explosiveness. He knows how to seize opportunities."

Agassi had done his best to do just that during the point, several times. Each time, with the crowd rumbling, ready to roar for Agassi, Sampras somehow stretched to reach shots, keeping the rally alive.

"[The shots] were good enough to win, but you're also expecting the ball to come back," Agassi said.

For both players, the struggle continued after the point, as each fought to catch his wind, and for a moment it was imaginable that the point and set, though gone, might pay an eventual dividend for Agassi. While he is not and never will be the athlete Sampras is, he was unquestionably in better condition at the time. Before hooking up with Brad Gilbert, Agassi's weight was a problem but his upper body surely wasn't. He pumped weights more than most players, giving him the barrel-chested look that is accented by those skinny, bandy legs that somehow short-step to every ball. The post-Gilbert Agassi has the endurance. Watching Sampras sag after winning the set, the image of Yzaga popped up in the mind's eye.

And then, it was gone. Sampras broke serve in the second game of the second set. He then settled into a serving performance reminiscent of the 1990 final, but with an update indicative of Sampras' maturing as a player and, more so, as a champion.

Three consecutive aces made it 4-1. Power ball. We'd seen it before. But then, in the ninth game, on set point, Sampras found the middle of the ad-court box with a 76-mph puff-ball that sliced away from Agassi. Sampras screamed after the shot. Agassi stalked off, to his seat.

Genius can be flaky, though, one reason it can be so compelling to watch. Sampras, a risk-taker by design, gets incredibly brave when he's ahead. Inherently convinced that he's unbeatable, one- or two-set advantages allow him to truly 'feel it'. But there is always the danger of breakdown. After all, has Sampras ever pushed a ball in his life? Gullikson used to talk about Laver's ability to swing away when things got tight, to "hit his way out of it". That's what Sampras does from the outset. It's a football kind of thing: the best form of defence is attack.

Up a service break at 2-1 in the third set, Sampras' offence finally sputtered. He double-faulted, then blew a half-volley, letting Agassi break back. Agassi broke again in the tenth game, winning the set when his best shot, a forehand return that neutralised a 122-mph Sampras serve, set up an even-larger fore-hand pass.

While Sampras lost the eventually crucial fourth game, you had to be impressed with Agassi. Winning the third set was yet another example of his turnaround under Gilbert. A few years earlier he would have been out of there after going two sets down.

"It's always tough to close out a match against a difficult opponent," Agassi said. "I felt like Pete still had to close me out even though he was up a couple of sets and a break. I wasn't planning on going anywhere. I was just trying to find a window of opportunity somewhere to get into the match. When I got the break in the fourth game I think that just elevated my intensity, and sucked out every last bit of anything that was inside of me."

Sampras was worried there was more.

"Andre started to get some confidence, won the third set and the crowd started really getting behind him," Sampras said. "But I was still up a set and I felt like he still had a long way to go to beat me. He's a tough guy to put away. You need to play at a high level for three straight sets, but I got a little tight. Maybe I saw the trophy in my hand."

Sampras' blurred vision cleared quickly in the fourth, even though he botched a break point in the opening game by flagging a routine forehand. He soon settled into serving another hot streak, peaking with four consecutive aces in the sixth game.

"You just get into a great groove," Sampras explained of his 'perfect' game, appropriately throwing in a baseball analogy: "It's like throwing three strikes. Everything just clicks and you start feeling that you can toss it up there and hit the line. That's what I have to do against Andre. If I don't hit a great serve he's going to make me volley. So I got a little bit lucky and snapped off a couple of good aces."

Agassi, judging by his hang-dog body language, had to know the end was near. Amazing that he wasn't broken until the 11th game, a break set up by a terribly hit double-fault at love–30. As Sampras walked back to serve the 12th game, was there any doubt?

Not on the first point, a 118-mph ace. Certainly not on the last, a 120-mile number up the centre — his 142nd ace of the tournament.

Agassi never flinched.

Sampras, at your service: 6-4, 6-3, 4-6, 7-5.

"It's a deceptive serve, no question," said Agassi, "but if you're hitting 123mph on the line it doesn't matter if the other guy knows where it's going or not. But more than his first serve, I didn't feel like I could swing freely at his second serve on the side where the wind was at your back. Something like six service games in a row when he served into the wind, he missed the first serve, put the second serve into the court and I hit returns that just floated long. But I think he served extremely well, too. He came up with some big first serves on some crucial break points. It's discouraging when his strength is going well but likewise, it's that way with anybody's strength."

Said Sampras: "I was surprised myself how well I served… because the conditions were so windy. My toss was all over the place. The serve was the one shot that kind of saved me."

At the post-match press conferences, two separate discussions developed with each player. One dealt with the day, with Agassi's contention that the long, hot summer and his 26-match victory streak leading up to the final had cost him. The other was big-picture, as both were asked about the world No.1 ranking still belonging to Agassi but, by all rights, should have been immediately transferred to Sampras — as with a boxing title fight, or a national championship college football bowl game.

It was hard to swallow Agassi's line that he was drained, that he had little left for the biggest match of the year, perhaps the biggest of his career. He had simply looked too good during the tournament, save for a second-round five-setter against Alex Corretja. But even then, the last two sets — 6-0, 6-2 — made up for losing two 7-5 sets.

"I think next summer I'm going to lose a little bit… I'd give up all 26 right now, to have the one back," Agassi said.

Sampras, though, partially validated Agassi's contention. In fact, prior to the Open, Sampras had almost predicted it. He had talked of 1992 and a good summer tour, two tournament titles, and then having nothing left by the time Stefan Edberg and he played the Open final.

Agassi said he felt like every match, except for the semi-final win over Becker, was a struggle. "The couple of days off before I played Boris really helped me a lot, but to come back and play today… I mean… in the first set after that long point, I felt my legs just… well, it was way too early in the match to be feeling the way I was feeling.

"But you can't not try when you play the summer tournaments. That's the price you pay to win a lot of matches. I guess I was lacking a little strength, a little pep in my step, so to speak. Before I played Becker, I felt like I had a little of my step back again. I just didn't quite have that little extra that I needed against Pete. But it's one-on-one out there, man. There ain't no hiding. I can't pass the ball."

Sampras did keep his concurring to a minimum, though. No way was he going to let the title be tainted. After all, he was tired, too.

"The fact that I played the first semi-final on Super Saturday and he played the second — he got done at 9pm — maybe he was a little bit fatigued at the end. He had a long summer. I felt pretty good."

Sampras then summed up the difference of the day, his words as cutting, as precise, as those serves had been:

"I felt this was a great opportunity;

"No time for excuses as far as being sore or tired;

"You need to suck it up;

"Do whatever you can."

How's that for four in a row?

So who was No.1? The rankings said one thing. Reality indicated something else. Sampras had won the season's last two Grand Slam tournaments. Agassi had won the first, the Australian

Open, had beaten Sampras three out of five times, and had the marvellous summer. Funny thing, the discussion that developed after this match. Agassi was more convinced that Sampras was No.1 than Sampras himself. Sampras made the point, though, that the primary ranking was secondary compared to the major titles, of which he now had seven.

"When you look back at the greatest players of all-time, you look at the numbers of Grand Slam tournaments they have won; the ranking is something everyone just takes for granted," he said. "In my mind the major titles are the most important thing; the fact that I won two really ends my year on a great note."

But Sampras also felt that the No.1 ranking should be tied to the majors, which makes sense.

"Your ranking should be a reflection of how you do at the majors. If you win a Wimbledon or a US Open, I think there should be a strong possibility that you should be No.1."

Agassi was on the same page, saying, "Pete has won two Slams so I'll have to say that come December 31 he's going to feel better about the year than I will. I just think that when your career is said and done, you want the Slams [to be your legacy]. I know what it's like to be No.1 and I know what it's like to win tournaments when you're No.1. You still want the Slams. Being No.1 is great but after the first hour it doesn't make a bit of difference because you still have every guy in the tournaments wanting to beat you. You want to peak for the big events. These are the ones you remember."

Sampras would remember this one, in part, as the one that renewed talk of his quest — unspoken but undeniable to have more Slam titles than anyone. His total of seven — three US Opens, three Wimbledons, one Australian Open — left him five behind Roy Emerson, four behind Bjorn Borg, but tied, at the age of 24, with McEnroe.

"Breaking the record isn't something I've really thought about," Sampras said. "I just see myself preparing the best I can for the majors, mentally and physically getting ready for each one. But it's not really something I put on a chalkboard: *I'm going to break Emerson's record.*"

Future US Opens will be crucial to Sampras' chances. Despite his overpowering Wimbledon performances, he continues to insist that a medium-paced hard court is his favourite surface. While New York represents all that he is not, he somehow acclimatises himself to the setting, almost thriving on it. One can envision Sampras using the Open as an anchor to his career as he approaches 30, much like Connors and McEnroe did.

He has won the tournament three times.

He could easily double that.

As Sampras advances, inevitably, toward Emmo's mark, he will inevitably admit it is indeed a cherished goal.

As a daily reminder, he might even get a chalkboard.

He'll have the US Open titles circled.

US Open Record: Pete Sampras

The US Open was the first Grand Slam tournament Pete Sampras played, and the first Grand Slam tournament that he won. He places the Open just behind Wimbledon in importance.

US Open Record

1988

First round	Lost to Jaime Yzaga	6-7, 6-7, 6-4, 7-5, 6-2

1989

First round	Defeated Augustin Moreno	6-3, 5-7, 6-4, 6-1
Second round	Defeated Mats Wilander	5-7, 6-3, 1-6, 6-1, 6-4
Third round	Defeated Jaime Yzaga	4-6, 6-4, 6-3, 6-3
Fourth round	Lost to Jay Berger	7-5, 6-2, 6-1

1990

First round	Defeated Dan Goldie	6-1, 7-5, 6-1
Second round	Defeated Peter Lundgren	6-4, 6-3, 6-3
Third round	Defeated Jakob Hlasek	6-3, 6-4, 6-1
Fourth round	Defeated Thomas Muster	6-7, 7-6, 6-4, 6-3
Quarter-finals	Defeated Ivan Lendl	6-4, 7-6, 3-6, 4-6, 6-2
Semi-finals	Defeated John McEnroe	6-2, 6-4, 3-6, 6-3
Final	Defeated Andre Agassi	6-4, 6-3, 6-2

1991

First round	Defeated Christo Van Rensburg	6-0, 6-3, 6-2
Second round	Defeated Wayne Ferreira	6-1, 6-2, 2-2, retired
Third round	Defeated Stephane Simian	7-6, 6-4, 6-7, 6-3
Fourth round	Defeated David Wheaton	3-6, 6-2, 6-2, 6-4
Quarter-finals	Lost to Jim Courier	6-2, 7-6, 7-6

1992

First round	Defeated David Dilucia	6-3, 7-5, 6-2
Second round	Defeated Martin Damm	7-5, 6-1, 6-2
Third round	Defeated Todd Martin	7-6, 2-6, 4-6, 7-5, 6-4
Fourth round	Defeated Guy Forget	6-3, 1-6, 1-6, 6-4, 6-3
Quarter-finals	Defeated Alexander Volkov	6-4, 6-1, 6-0
Semi-finals	Defeated Jim Courier	6-1, 3-6, 6-2, 6-2
Final	Lost to Stefan Edberg	3-6, 6-4, 7-6, 6-2

1993

First round	Defeated Fabrice Santoro	6-3, 6-1, 6-2
Second round	Defeated Daniel Vacek	6-4, 5-7, 6-2, 7-6
Third round	Defeated Arnaud Boetsch	6-4, 6-3, 6-1
Fourth round	Defeated Thomas Enqvist	6-4, 6-4, 7-6
Quarter-finals	Defeated Michael Chang	6-7, 7-6, 6-1, 6-1
Semi-finals	Defeated Alexander Volkov	6-4, 6-3, 6-2
Final	Defeated Cedric Pioline	6-4, 6-4, 6-3

1994

First round	Defeated Kevin Ullyett	6-2, 6-2, 6-2
Second round	Defeated Daniel Vacek	6-3, 6-4, 6-4
Third round	Defeated Roger Smith	4-6, 6-2, 6-4, 6-3
Fourth round	Lost to Jaime Yzaga	3-6, 6-3, 4-6, 7-6, 7-5

1995

First round	Defeated Fernando Meligeni	6-0, 6-3, 6-4
Second round	Defeated Jaime Yzaga	6-1, 6-4, 6-3
Third round	Defeated Mark Philippoussis	6-7, 7-5, 7-5, 6-3
Fourth round	Defeated Todd Martin	7-6, 6-3, 6-4
Quarter-finals	Defeated Byron Black	7-6, 6-4, 6-0
Semi-finals	Defeated Jim Courier	7-5, 4-6, 6-4, 7-5
Final	Defeated Andre Agassi	6-4, 6-3, 4-6, 7-5

1996

First round	Defeated Jimy Szymanski	6-2, 6-2, 6-1
Second round	Defeated Jiri Novak	6-3, 1-6, 6-3, 4-6, 6-4
Third round	Defeated Alexander Volkov	6-3, 6-4, 6-2
Fourth round	Defeated Mark Philippoussis	6-3, 6-3, 6-4
Quarter-finals	Defeated Alex Corretja	7-6 (7-5), 5-7, 5-7, 6-4, 7-6 (9-7)
Semi-finals	Defeated Goran Ivanisevic	6-3, 6-4, 5-7 (9-11), 6-3
Final	Defeated Michael Chang	6-1, 6-4, 7-6 (7-3)

Career won-lost: 44-5

Sampras-Agassi: Head To Head

Pete Sampras has the overall edge on Andre Agassi, but their seven-year rivalry is marked by epic struggles at big events, including five meetings in Grand Slam tournaments.

Sampras–Agassi
As of August 1996: Sampras 10, Agassi 8

Tournament	Surface	Winner	Score
1989 Italian Open	Clay	Agassi	6-2, 6-1
1990 US Indoor	Carpet	Sampras	5-7, 7-5, retired
1990 US Open	Hard	Sampras	6-4, 6-3, 6-2
1990 ATP Tour Championships	Carpet	Agassi	6-4, 6-2
1991 ATP Tour Championships	Carpet	Sampras	6-3, 1-6, 6-3
1992 AT&T Challenge	Clay	Agassi	7-5, 6-4
1992 French Open	Clay	Agassi	7-6, 6-2, 6-1
1993 Wimbledon	Grass	Sampras	6-2, 6-2, 3-6, 3-6, 6-4
1994 Lipton Championships	Hard	Sampras	5-7, 6-3, 6-3
1994 Salem Open	Hard	Sampras	6-3, 6-1
1994 Paris Indoor	Carpet	Agassi	7-6, 7-5
1994 ATP Tour Championships	Carpet	Sampras	4-6, 7-6, 6-3
1 995 Australian Open	Hard	Agassi	4-6, 6-1, 7-6, 6-4
1995 Champions Cup	Hard	Sampras	7-5, 6-3, 7-5
1995 Lipton Championships	Hard	Agassi	3-6, 6-2, 7-6
1995 Canadian Open	Hard	Agassi	3-6, 6-2, 6-3
1995 US Open	Hard	Sampras	6-4, 6-3, 4-6, 7-5
1996 Sybase Open	Hard	Sampras	6-2, 6-3

How Sampras Goes To War

Pete Sampras' accessories — racquet, clothing, shoes — always have complemented his game. Sampras is classic, all around, starting with his racquet, a Wilson Pro Staff Mid, which he has used for the last nine years. The model, with its smaller-than-average mid-sized hitting surface, offers perhaps the closest modern-day approximation to the feel of the old wooden racquets. It is an unforgiving piece with a limited sweet spot that rewards only those with the talent to find it.

Today's Pro Staff is the high-tech, graphite-laden descendant of the original Wilson racquet by the same name that was a stiffer-than-normal slice of white ash conducive to control but lacking the power of say, the more flexible Wilson Jack Kramer of those days.

Sampras' choice of string? What many players, for decades, have considered the best: VS gut. Strung extra tight, it completes the precision package that allows Sampras to hit all out. He relies on his racquet to reel his power in, without compromising his stroke.

As far as clothing and shoes, Sampras started his professional career clad in Sergio Tacchini, head to toe. Several years ago he switched to Nike, partly because of what he considered its superior footwear; Sampras was looking to switch shoes after a rash of foot injuries.

Both companies have outfitted Sampras in tasteful attire befitting his low-key image and desire to emulate other eras' players, with his series of Nike lines purposely contrasting to the outlandish Nike outfits worn by Andre Agassi.

Sampras' Stick: Wilson Pro Staff Mid

Hitting area: 85 sq ins
Weight: 1³⁄₈oz
Main/cross strings: 16/18
String: VS gut
String tension: 74–80lbs (varies)
Grip size: 4⁷⁄₈ins
Extras: Tourna-Grip; 'String-a-lings' as string dampeners; 1¹⁄₈oz of strategically placed lead tape.

Part II
Davis Cup

The Red

Scare 5

S MART-ASS Russians.
  Having reached the Davis Cup final for the second consecutive year, they started talking about winning it long
before the first ball was struck on their carefully constructed red-
clay court, the focal point of a grand plan to become 'world
champions'.

And certainly, the United States team, particularly Pete
Sampras, looked vulnerable to this tactic.

As were the Germans. That's why the Olympic Stadium, an
indoor arena in Moscow, had been turned into a mud-bog,
monster-truck race course in late September for the Russia-
Germany semi-final. Then, just to be funny, the Russians put
some lines down, and strung a net across the muck. And laid in
wait for serve-and-volleyers Boris Becker and Michael Stich to
walk on to the water-soaked surface, sink in and take their
country's Davis Cup hopes down with them.

It almost backfired. Despite the quicksand, Becker and Stich
won the opening-day singles from Andrei Chesnokov and Yevgeny
Kafelnikov, thought to have an edge on slow clay, a bigger edge on

mud. The court had been deemed unplayable by referee Gilbert Ysern prior to play; it clearly had been doctored to dent the Germans' power games. It smacked of the old days in major league baseball, when groundsmen would saturate parts of the playing area to counter certain strengths in the home club's line-up.

The International Tennis Federation didn't care for it. They fined the Russians $25,000. Ysern actually delayed the start of the first day's play so the court could dry out. Hair-dryers were borrowed from a nearby hotel, extension cords brought out and, of course, the effect was minimal.

For the rest of the weekend, the court was in better shape but inexplicably, the Russians were, too. They won the middle-day doubles to close at 2-1. Then, with Becker out due to a back injury, German substitute Bernd Karbacher lost to Kafelnikov and Stich blew nine match points in losing to Chesnokov.

The other semi-final, featuring the Swedes and the US, in Agassi's hometown of Las Vegas, was an emotional ride for Sampras. Tim Gullikson, during an upbeat time in his fight against brain cancer, was able to attend and even spent some time at courtside at the invitation of his brother Tom, the US team captain. Sampras won both his singles to key a 4-1 victory.

On to Moscow, in the first week of December, and the same patch of red clay. At least the Americans could count on a fair surface. The ITF's Davis Cup committee gave the All Russia Tennis Association a stern warning that similar high jinks in the future could result in losing the home-court advantage for at least one, maybe several, competitions. Home court in Davis Cup is the ultimate advantage, so it was safe to assume the court would be kosher this time around.

Still, that didn't stop the Russians from talking big, upon notification of the United States line-up of Sampras and Courier in singles, Todd Martin and Richey Reneberg in doubles. Sampras' relative weakness on clay prompted Kafelnikov to say he feared Courier — a two-time French Open champion — far more on clay. Kafelnikov went on to posit that the US was virtually conceding the doubles point. Chesnokov chimed in, saying his side had a '50-50' chance since Sampras was playing.

It should be noted that Sampras, at the time, was 3-0 against Kafelnikov 1-0 against Chesnokov.

Sampras originally was to play doubles only, with Martin. Then Agassi reaggravated a chest muscle that he first injured in Las Vegas, which forced him to sit out the semi-final against Sweden, giving way to Martin, who provided the clinching point. Sampras, in an indication of how badly he wanted to help the Cup cause, agreed with Gullikson's view that he should give way to Courier and Agassi in singles.

The United States Tennis Association announced Agassi's withdrawal on a Tuesday, only three days before the final was to begin. That dented Gullikson's optimism, at first buoyed by having 'the strongest team possible'.

"To be honest," Gullikson said, "I was hoping to have Andre but I wasn't expecting it. It's clear he hasn't been well since the semi-finals, or he would have been playing."

Agassi had won his last 13 Davis Cup singles matches, tying McEnroe's 1981-82 streak, and was 22-4 overall. Russian captain Anatoli Lepeshin said his side was 'relieved' that Agassi — who showed up to support his team-mates — was out.

No wonder the Russians feared Courier. He looked like a lucky charm. Even though he was only 9-5 in Davis Cup singles, the US was 7-0 with him in the line-up; he also carried a seven-match winning streak dating back to the 1992 final, which he clinched by beating Switzerland's Jakob Hlasek.

Upon Agassi's withdrawal, Sampras, who had reassumed his No.1 world ranking several weeks earlier, quickly adjusted his focus, despite his history of mediocre Davis Cup performances: Coming into the 1995 World Group competition he had a 5-5 record, starting with his infamous Davis Cup debut, a two-defeat collapse against France in the 1991 final. Four victories in 1995 made it look better on paper but the fact remained that he was an unproven Cup commodity.

"I'll just have to put on my clay-court shoes, go out and do it," Sampras said upon arrival in Moscow. "Hopefully I can pull one out of my hat on the red clay. The court is playing pretty slow, which isn't great for me. But it is the same for both sides."

And, since Sampras was available, Gullikson already was pondering the prospect of using him in singles and doubles, which, of course, would really be pushing the clay-court envelope.

"We have several different options but I told Pete it could come down to him playing both," Gullikson said. "We could change the doubles and add Pete if we have to."

Sampras didn't care for that initially, saying, "I don't know how excited I would be to play three days in a row. Since I'm now going to play singles I would prefer not to play doubles. If I have one day of rest between the two singles, physically I'll feel better."

Thus, a strange atmosphere prevailed as the competition approached. The United States had won more Davis Cup titles, 30, than any other country. No Russian/Soviet team had won even one. The US was in its 58th final. The Russians were in their second, having lost to Sweden in 1994.

Sampras was ranked No.1 in the world, Courier at No.8. Kafelnikov was No.6, but Chesnokov was down at No.91. As for the other Russian, doubles specialist Andrei Olhovskiy, well, suffice it to say he wasn't to be feared.

Yet the Americans were talking cautiously, and the Russians, well, they were just talking.

"I believe the choice of clay gives us a good opportunity, maybe the only opportunity, to win the Davis Cup against the US team," Kafelnikov said the day before play began. "It's a big advantage for us."

Meanwhile, there was something brewing, deep within the soul of Sampras. A rich mixture of emotions.

It was part Gullikson — coach Tim, whose condition back home in Illinois was worsening; and captain Tom, who had dealt with the same daily anguish all year while trying to keep the Cup effort together.

It was part redemption — no matter what Sampras said at the time, the spectre of 1991, in Lyon, when he crumbled under the pressure of playing for his nation in a hostile atmosphere, haunted him. And since, he had been no great shakes in Davis Cup, so-so at best.

It was, finally, part validation — Sampras had regained the No.1 ranking from Agassi, but just as he had lost it by the whim of the ATP Tour's computer points system, so had he regained it. The Davis Cup awarded no points. Only honour. What better note to end the year on?

"The situational importance of this setting, this was a time Pete could really show who he was," said California journalist Mark Winters, who has written about Sampras since he was a nine-year-old junior prodigy.

"You see, this Davis Cup," added Winters, "was Pete's Cup."

Le Choke 6

THE TENNIS WORLD, for the most part, loves Davis Cup. Delete America. That fact isn't lost on the American players who visit foreign soil, experience the all-for-one atmosphere and wonder what the hell's going on back home. Davis Cup in the United States is sometimes a tough sell, particularly when the team is missing a Sampras or an Agassi.

Maybe that's a partial explanation, or an excuse, for America's occasional stumbles away from home. Agassi has always yearned for American fans to get with it. "To be honest, I'd like to take the Davis Cup to a place like Athens, Georgia," Agassi said, referring to the University of Georgia stadium where the NCAA men's championships are played, generally before raucous, vocal crowds.

"It'd be good to get some of those, er, Southerners involved. A college town. Where they sell beer. That would suit me. But of course, there are other considerations."

Agassi said all that during one of the most somnambulistic Davis Cup weekends in history, a quarter-final against Czechoslovakia in Fort Myers, Florida, where the dance of the living dead is ongoing, especially at high-brow events like Davis Cup where the median age is 65 and folks get injured falling off their wallets. To get such crowds excited, consumption of one double-espresso should be mandatory upon entry. Ban bottled water, which may well be the bane of American tennis crowds. Make it double-bourbon for everyone.

"Our crowds tend to be less nationalistic," said USTA communications department official Art Campbell. "Our crowds support our guys, but just not as enthusiastically bordering on crazed, as you see in Europe."

So many times, then, American players are ill-prepared for an out-of-country experience. And it doesn't have to be a coin-throwing crowd like that encountered in 1987 in Asuncion, Paraguay, when a 3-2 loss knocked the US out of the competition. Nationalistic fervour is sufficient to unnerve anyone. A newcomer to Davis Cup? Especially at risk. In Davis Cup history, only four American players had made singles debuts in the final. Three had lost. Only McEnroe, in 1978, had escaped the curse, beating Britain's John Lloyd.

So what was Pete Sampras doing in Lyon, France, in November 1991? He didn't know then. He still doesn't.

Wrong place, wrong time. Sampras stepped into the path of destiny that weekend. But who could have known?

US Cup captain Tom Gorman chose Sampras and Agassi, and rightfully. Sampras was ranked No.6 and was the hottest player in the world at the time, 36-6 since August. Agassi, 11-4 in Davis Cup play, was a given. Nothing wrong with those choices. Sure, there was concern about Sampras, but that was unavoidable as was his selection. Besides, whatever misgivings existed had to do with doubles. Gorman had named Ken Flach and Robbie Seguso as his team, bypassing McEnroe, who had lobbied heavily for a spot on the squad.

France, as its top player Guy Forget noted, has three sporting events that truly excite its populous: World Cup, the Tour de France and the Davis Cup. The French have never let go of its glory years, the years when the Four Musketeers — Rene Lacoste, Henri Cochet, Jean Borotra and Jacques Brugnon — rode roughshod over tennis. Those four had won the Cup in 1927 beating the Americans, then kept the Cup for five years before a loss in 1933 to England.

It had been hard times, since, with France appearing only once more in the final, in 1982, losing 4-1 to a McEnroe-led American team.

At the 8,300-seat Palais de Sport in Lyon, the French installed a quick Supreme indoor court, favourable to Sampras and Agassi but also to the flashy, attacking home-team players, Forget and Henri Leconte. Coming into the competition, the 31-year-old Leconte looked like the key. Only four months removed from having back surgery, his world ranking down to 159th, there was no reason to expect him to play well. At the same time, there was every reason to figure he would find a way to do so.

The US got an apparent break when the order of play was determined: Agassi and Forget matched in the opening singles, followed by Sampras-Leconte.

"I'm hoping Andre will go out and win and calm down the crowd," said Sampras. "That will help me a little bit."

"I'm happy it turned out this way," Agassi said. "I'm comfortable with it, because I know what to expect out there more than Pete. I think there are a few more nerves involved when you play first. I've done it a few times already. I think this can help us to get an early lead."

Captain of the French team, Yannick Noah, no longer active as a player, was still scoring with head games. At the draw, he tabbed Arnaud Boetsch to play doubles with Forget; Flach and Seguso scoffed, saying Noah would certainly switch to Leconte. Noah even suggested he might play doubles. The ITF said no, he wouldn't, since he wasn't declared eligible before the draw commenced.

No, if there was going to be a substitution, it would be Leconte, one of the game's fabulous shot-makers gearing for a final run, hoping to win back the adulation of the French crowds, who had forsaken him somewhat as his results had waned.

"Henri is the type of player who can beat anyone, anywhere," Noah said. "He has been so close to being dead. Now he's coming back to life. I believe he's going to give everything he can."

Sampras never had a chance.

Agassi won the kick-off against Forget, running through the last three sets after dropping the first in a tie-break, giving Sampras all the help he could. Two hours and 24 minutes later, the competition was tied 1-1. Leconte's straight-set victory exposed Sampras as a rookie unprepared for the Davis Cup experience.

"It was a different feeling from any I've had on the court," Sampras said. "So many things were going on in my mind that I've never had going on before. It was a tough experience."

It got tougher. Noah, of course, changed up and put Leconte in the doubles. He had to. Boetsch wasn't near the complete player he is today and besides, Flach and Seguso — Wimbledon doubles champions in 1987-88 — were 7-0 against French teams.

After beating Sampras, Leconte said he couldn't remember playing a more complete match. He could have said the same thing after the doubles. He and Forget won in four sets. Leconte was a Euro-Connors, pumping his fist after hitting winners, inciting the crowd into rhythmic clapping, flag-waving, chants of 'Henri'.

Before the competition started, Flach had said the pressure was on the French, because they were at home. Now, the pressure had shifted squarely to Sampras' increasingly slumping shoulders, mainly because he was an ill-equipped 20-year-old who was not at home.

Sampras had played Forget, a multi-faceted left-hander, several weeks earlier in the Paris Open final. Forget won in five sets. Forget also had downed Sampras in August, at the ATP Championships. So it didn't look good for the American, not with 8,000 partisans jeering at his every move, cheering his every error.

Whatever Leconte had, it rubbed off on Forget. He served 17 aces, many at absolutely critical times, to beat Sampras in four sets and touch off a wild, extended celebration that Noah recorded with his video camera. Noah and Leconte then led the team in a conga-line dance around the arena. French President Francois Mitterrand sent a hasty telegram congratulating the team.

He should have sent one to Sampras, too.

Because, for all the warm-and-fuzzy Frenchness, Leconte's heroics, Forget's clutch serving, the weekend amounted to a serious gag. Sampras fanned, leaving Agassi ready to take centre-stage.

"I just wasn't ready," Sampras said later.

Making Up Is Hard To Do 7

LIVING with Lyon. That's what Sampras faced from the moment Forget blocked that forehand volley into an open court, then flopped on his back. Sampras was caught in the Davis Cup quandary that snags an American now and then. You want to play, kind of. Then, suddenly, you're in waist-deep, against somebody who inherently has far more motivation churning in his soul than you. And if you falter, a surprise emotional toll surfaces. For something you didn't really care about that much to begin with, the Davis Cup can become all-encompassing, probably more so upon failing.

"The Americans didn't realise how much the Davis Cup meant to the French people and the French team," Forget said.

Having been indoctrinated, Sampras immediately committed to making things right. Two weeks after the 1991 final, he was named in the United States team, along with Agassi, that would face Argentina in a first-round 1992 match in Hawaii.

On an outdoor hard court, with a sun-baked crowd that reminded him of his California roots, Sampras defeated Martin Jaite in four sets and Alberto Mancini in two, the latter victory a 'dead rubber' — Davis Cup terminology for a match played after a competition has been decided — in a 5-0 US shutout.

It was just what Sampras needed, after Lyon, to regain his Davis Cup bearings, and led to his being named to the quarter-final squad against the Czechs, in Fort Myers. This was the weekend when Sampras stood in awe of Agassi and looked awesome himself in straight-setting Karel Novacek; Agassi's pummelling of Petr Korda put the US up 2-0.

"I think this was the first day I've really felt comfortable on the court in Davis Cup [since Lyon]," Sampras said. "This was a little bit of [redemption]."

The next day, though, saw the heavily favoured US doubles team of McEnroe and Rick Leach play miserably — Leach, mainly — in losing to Korda and Cyril Suk. That shifted the pressure to Sampras, scheduled to start the last day's play by facing Korda.

Struggling with his serve, victimised by one of Korda's hot streaks he was so capable of at the time, Sampras went down in four sets. The two-hour, 17-minute match was Lyon revisited. Thankfully, Agassi was up to the challenge, blitzing Novacek in straights, 6-0 scores in the last two sets.

"I really wanted Pete to win for him," Agassi said. "I also didn't want the momentum swing to continue as it had started to when we lost the doubles. We spent a day and a half feeling like we were going to win [easily]. When it gets this close, though, anything is possible.

"The feeling was very discouraging when Pete lost. I felt positive about my match, but there's only so much you can do."

Gorman switched up for the next round against Sweden. In a rare move by an American side hosting a competition, he chose red clay as the surface, laid down in the unlikely setting of the Target Center in Minneapolis. Rare, but right on, and tied to his singles selections — Agassi and Jim Courier. Courier had won a second consecutive French Open title four months earlier; Agassi was the French runner-up in 1990-91.

Sampras and McEnroe were to be paired in doubles, an interesting tandem but precarious, considering their dislike for clay and the fact that Sampras and Davis Cup were starting to look like oil and water. Gorman was handed another problem: his prospective team looked bad in practice, bad enough to make the him contemplate a last-minute change, perhaps using Courier, most likely with McEnroe.

What a talent-laden competition. Stefan Edberg, who had defeated Sampras in the US Open final two weeks earlier, was ranked No.1 in the world. Courier, Sampras and Agassi were 2, 3 and 6, respectively. And McEnroe, all-time Davis Cup victory leader.

Day one, Agassi defeated Edberg and Courier beat Nicklas Kulti for a 2-0 lead. Day two, Sampras and McEnroe clinched with a five-set victory over Edberg and Anders Jarryd, a match marred by one severe Sampras hiccup. With the match tied at a set apiece, and Sampras serving at 4-5, he double-faulted, giving the Swedes the set. Any sign of shakiness on Sampras' part was duly noted, but at least forgiven this time.

The final against Switzerland, on a hard court in Fort Worth, Texas, brought the same four Americans together. When the first day singles resulted in a split — Courier lost to past nemesis Marc Rosset, while Agassi beat Jakob Hlasek — the doubles point became imperative.

Sampras found himself on the end of a classic McEnroe outburst, but one occurring in the locker room, during their doubles match. Having dropped the first two sets in tie-breakers to Rosset and Hlasek, the Americans broke Rosset in the 12th game of the third set to win 7-5. The 10-minute break that followed featured approximately eight minutes of Mac, who had supplied the break by crushing a forehand return.

"He was getting pumped up, saying, 'let's kick some ass'; it was on that level," Sampras said. "He was so pumped, just ranting and raving, that we went out there [afterward] and played some extremely good tennis."

As in 6-1, 6-2, good for a 2-1 US lead. Courier played sporadically the next afternoon in beating Hlasek over four sets, but it was enough to clinch and allow Sampras to feel good about himself for the second consecutive competition.

Sampras begged off Davis Cup in 1993, saying he wanted to concentrate on achieving the No.1 world ranking. He realised that goal on April 12, becoming the 11th player to do so since the rankings began in 1973.

The other top players also took a break from the first round, leaving Brad Gilbert and David Wheaton to travel to Australia. The US was summarily dismissed.

Having declared himself back in the mix in 1994, Sampras travelled to Rotterdam for a quarter-final against The Netherlands, a decision he rues to this day and one that would affect all his future Davis Cup commitments.

After a month on grass courts topped by a second consecutive Wimbledon championship, the sudden switch to hard courts for the quarter-final proved a bad move. Sampras' left ankle became inflamed with tendinitis during the weekend. He beat Jacco Eltingh but lost to another big server, Richard Krajicek. That left the score 2-2 entering the decisive singles, won by Courier over Eltingh.

Sampras returned home to Tampa figuring his summer was in trouble. The ankle did not heal, at least not well enough for him to return to tournament competition. His cardiovascular level fell off, and he lost to Yzaga.

A week after the Open, Vitas Gerulaitis was found dead, from apparent carbon monoxide poisoning. Gerulaitis and Sampras had become good friends, and the loss hit hard. Yet, when Sampras was called upon for the semi-final in late September, against Sweden in Gothenberg, he was there. As was Vitas, in spirit; all the US team members wore a letter 'V' on their shirts, as a memorial.

Sampras defeated Magnus Larsson on the first day. Coupled with Todd Martin's upset of Edberg, the US went up 2-0. But seldom do Davis Cup victories come easily, an unwritten rule that Sampras knows all too well. He watched teammates Jared Palmer and Jon Stark lose to Jan Apell and Jonas Bjorkman in four sets, grimacing at the thought of the next day counting.

Sampras had strained his right hamstring against Larsson. After dropping the first set to Edberg 6-3, Sampras retired, leaving another competition deadlocked at 2-2. Martin — like Sampras three years before — wasn't up to it. He played tentatively in losing the decider to Larsson. The Swedes' 3-2 victory sent them to the final, in which they defeated Russia.

Sampras' injury couldn't be helped. "It was pretty apparent he was hobbling," recalls the USTA's Campbell. Another unfortunate Davis Cup experience, but for once, he had an out.

Real or not, though, the retirement further marred Sampras' record as the only one in Davis Cup history that came in a match that mattered to a competition's outcome.

Pete The Great 8

T HE Russians had a plan for dealing with Sampras in December 1995. They wanted to expose his sometimes questionable stamina; do that, they figured, and his clay court game, equally questionable, would also be exposed.

Sampras had won a total of 36 tournaments in his career; two had come on clay — the 1994 Italian Open and Kitzbuhel, 1992. Seven of the 36 were Grand Slams, but Sampras had never won the French Open and didn't look like he ever would after losing in the first round of the 1995 event to Gilbert Schaller, that after a long spring red-clay campaign.

Both singles were going to be tough. Kafelnikov for obvious reasons, as he had quickly become one of the world's top players since turning professional in 1992. At the age of 21 his future was bright, his tone bold. Sampras' 3-0 edge commenced with a monumental victory in the fourth round of the 1994 Australian Open, Sampras prevailing 9-7 in the fifth set. Sampras' other two victories were in the 1994 World Team Cup and the 1995 ATP Finals, the former on clay, an encouraging sign, the latter coming just two weeks before, on an indoor carpet obviously favouring Sampras.

Chesnokov was ranked 91st, but not much was made of that,

since 1995 would be the first year he would finish out of the top 50 since 1987. A winner of seven tournaments, Chesnokov can be most effective on clay, where his retrieving qualities are of particular value. "Chesnokov," said Mark Winters, "is the Arantxa Sanchez Vicario of men's professional tennis."

Sampras and Chesnokov were drawn to open the competition. The match played out perfectly for the Russians. Sampras led two sets to one, then closed in on victory, leading 4-2 in the fourth, 40-15 on his serve. Somehow, though, Chesnokov won the fourth set in a tie-break.

Sampras was playing nervously, feeling the burden of leading the team with Agassi out. Chesnokov was playing his game, which consists of running down virtually every shot, giving the opponent every chance to beat himself.

"I thought Chesnokov was out of miracles after the semi-finals, but he tried to pull another one off," Tom Gullikson said.

The final set's sixth game was key. It lasted 17 points, but Sampras held his serve for 3-3. Sampras then started to cramp. A hamstring went first. But still he managed a service break to lead 5-4.

"This was a great competitive match," Winters recalled. "At the changeovers you could see Pete's legs were going. Even his movements between points looked very funny. He started doing deep knee bends. Pete doesn't play methodically but during this match he did, becoming almost Chesnokov-like in his movements."

Until the last game.

"It was, well, enthralling," Winters said. "Pete hit winners. He had to hit winners. Then the game is over and all of a sudden they're dragging him off the court."

Within seconds of the last point in Sampras' 3-6, 6-4, 6-3, 6-7, 6-4 win, he collapsed, his muscles entangled by cramps. Immediately, further contribution on his part looked doubtful. But after a muscle relaxer, massage and fluids, he bounced back, and appeared surprisingly nonchalant at the post-match interview, considering what he'd been through.

"I thought I made things a little more difficult than I should have," Sampras said. "I was smelling the victory up 4-2 and 40-15 and let him off the hook. Then I played an impatient tie-breaker.

"Andrei has all the ingredients to play well on the [red clay]. And I knew coming into the match that I was going to be the guy to win or lose it because he was going to let me play. The last couple of games I put a couple of good shots together and that was it."

That was it, and that was that — until several hours later when Courier had been blown off court in straight sets by Kafelnikov.

Kafelnikov's arrogance resurfaced. He said the event would be decided by the doubles. And he was already on record, regarding how the doubles would go.

Sampras went back to the hotel. Ate steak and potatoes. That was Bjorn Borg's meal of choice during his best days. But the symbolism cannot be overlooked: good old-fashioned American food served up in the heart of Russia, even if it was a Russia of the post-Cold War 1990s that had all the glitz and detachment as, say, a Las Vegas.

Sampras' meal fortified his soul probably more than his body; nothing like a big hunk of red meat the night before three hours of physical activity.

But he would need both body and soul for what was ahead.

The Russians must have slept well. They had knocked off Courier. And it sure looked as if they'd decimated Sampras. As they dozed, dreams of Todd Martin danced in their heads.

Kafelnikov and his coach/captain, Anatoli Lepeshin, got out early on the Saturday morning before the doubles. They were shocked to see Sampras practising already with Vince Spadea, an up-and-coming player from Boca Raton, Florida, chosen by Gullikson as a sparring partner for the final.

"Kafelnikov and his coach both had this 'holy shit' look on their faces when they saw Pete hitting," Winters said.

Sampras told Gullikson he was stiff but ready to play. Gullikson made the change, subbing Sampras for Reneberg. Was there a choice? Not in Gullikson's view. He had the world's No.1-ranked player and by God, he was going to use him.

"Pete sucked it up and said, 'I'll play if you really want me to'," Gullikson said.

Due to the 11th-hour decision, Gullikson had to loan Sampras a couple of white Nike shirts for the match. He didn't care.

After some early stumbles by Martin, he and Sampras ran off three sets against Kafelnikov and Olhovskiy. Remember all the talk about weak links? In this match, that label was reserved for Kafelnikov.

Winters thinks the moment when Kafelnikov first saw Sampras had an effect on the doubles outcome. "I have no doubt about that," Winters said. "I think the Russians were psyched out. Kafelnikov was basically out of the match very early on. He was flagging balls."

Kafelnikov still was a hard sell. Martin's serve was broken to start the match. Kafelnikov read too much into that. At least he admitted as much later. Was he going down hard, or what?

"After the first game I relaxed too much," he said. "I probably underestimated my opponents."

Gullikson, like almost anyone who knows tennis, found it hard to believe anyone, at any time, could ever underestimate Pete Sampras.

"I'm well aware what a gifted player the guy is," Gullikson said. "Any time you can put him on the court, you do it."

Kafelnikov's serve was broken twice in the first set, four times overall. "Once we got into it they made a couple of mistakes and we started playing better," said Martin, marvellous down the stretch.

"I was pretty much spent after [the singles]," Sampras said "But this is the Davis Cup, the final and we want to hold the Cup up [in triumph]. I was prepared to do whatever it takes. Once the adrenalin kicks in you don't worry about what you're feeling."

Added Martin: "It was good for me to know that Pete didn't have much energy to waste because it made me work harder, and it was good for him because it made him very efficient."

The US was up 2-1, but its chances remained dubious if you listened to Kafelnikov, who bounced back from the doubles loss by spouting off, yet again, his original strategy.

"After [his singles match] I know that Sampras' drawback is that he cannot stay on the court very long," Kafelnikov said. "So, the longer I can play, the better."

No American had won three matches on a Davis Cup weekend since John McEnroe in 1982. But now, there was every indication that it could happen again, with one, crucial qualifier. Sampras needed to play something akin to hard-court tennis against Kafelnikov.

There was wisdom in the Russian's wisecracks. Sampras had to run out of gas at some point. A fast start and relatively fast points throughout were imperative.

With another crowd of 14,000 watching, Sampras came out and continued where he had left off against Chesnokov. Showing the right amount of patience, Sampras jumped on his opportunities, stunning Kafelnikov with outright winners. And always, there was the serve, 16 aces this time.

Sampras raced through two sets, 6-2, 6-4. Then, finally, he started to show the effects of his efforts, stretching his sore hamstring between points, letting the occasional Kafelnikov shot go without a chase.

He ended the third-set tie-breaker with an ace. Kafelnikov, at last, was out of words. "He didn't give me a chance," he said in English before confronting a cadre of Russian reporters ready with questions about his inability to back up his boasts.

"The best clay-court match I ever played," was Sampras' summation.

"I've never seen better tennis for the first two sets," Gullikson said. "Pete couldn't have picked a bigger moment than the Davis Cup final."

"Pete took Kafelnikov out of the match immediately," Winters said. "Kafelnikov would hit a forehand, Pete would launch a forehand. If Pete had been more physically able, it would have been worse."

"The Russians looked at me as the weak link," Sampras said. "To come in and play on my worst surface against tough opponents and a very tough crowd was difficult. But I think I can play some good tennis on clay. You have to, to beat Andrei and Yevgeny."

"These were the best matches I've ever seen him play," added Winters, who believed that Sampras' motivation was rooted in the past — Lyon, his history of bombing on red clay, his affinity for the Gulliksons — more than the present.

The Russians might have seemed cocky, but Sampras hardly noticed.

"I don't think Pete plays into that kind of stuff," Winters said. "However, he had a point to prove. You know, to beat the home boy on his turf, to crush him, to rub his face into it… that had to be kind of sweet."

Courier dropped the last, insignificant match to Chesnokov, and the US team headed back to its hotel for another traditional American feast: Pizza and beer.

Funny thing about Davis Cup. As soon as one round is decided, captains and players are immediately besieged by questions about the next round, or in the case of the post-final discussions, about the next year.

Gullikson barely had time to savour Sampras' heroics, which gave the United States its 31st title, when a 1996 prospectus was requested by the media in Moscow.

Already, he had some ominous-sounding news.

"I know Pete wants to take the first [competition] off and it's well-deserved," Gullikson said. "The Cup is back in America where it belongs. Next year is complicated by the Olympics; that crowds an already-crowded schedule. My goal is to get all the top players involved."

Oops.

Gullikson had problems getting virtually any of the top players involved in 1996. The US thumped Mexico 5-0 in the first round, with Michael Chang and Todd Martin playing singles. But a quarter-final trip to Prague, in April, ended in elimination. In place of the previous December's powerhouse, Gullikson took a singles line-up comparable to a major league baseball team's eight and nine hitters: Martin and Mal Washington. Patrick McEnroe and Patrick Galbraith, the doubles team, actually looked like the line-up's strength, which shows the predicament Gullikson was in.

The Czechs presented a two-man team of Petr Korda and Daniel Vacek. Martin played heroically, beating both in singles. Washington lost twice, including the decisive match that gave the Czechs the 3–2 upset.

Various factors contributed to the 'B' team. Courier wanted to start preparation for the French Open. Agassi was busy filming a commercial and although that came off looking bad, it was hard to slam him too much given his record of success. Chang? Off to Asia, as was Sampras. Both also eyed the French.

But all seemed to share a common dismay over the never-ending, unyielding commitment Davis Cup requires. Sampras and Agassi were the most outspoken; with both planning to play in the 1996 Olympics — Sampras withdrew with an Achilles tendon injury — they shared the belief that Davis Cup should take a break during an Olympic year.

Sampras had another reason for backing off. The injury suffered during the summer of 1994, against the Dutch, had led to the US Open/Yzaga disaster. Just as nothing excites Sampras like the prospect of winning a major championship, nothing bothers him more than a blown opportunity. Davis Cup cost him dearly in 1994.

"I've really paid the price [for playing] in some ways," Sampras said in late March 1996, during the Lipton Championships, a week before the second-round debacle.

"This year I wasn't planning on playing the first two rounds. It just wasn't going to work out for me — going to Asia right after Lipton. If I were to pull it off [for the second round] I'd have to go to Lipton, Europe, Asia, then back to the States. That's just too much tennis. I remember the last thing I wanted to do after I lost the Lipton final [in 1995] was hop on a plane and go to Palermo. But it worked out pretty well at the end.

"In my mind, in an Olympic year I don't think Davis Cup should be played. I've always strongly felt Davis Cup should be played every two years. As far as getting more attention, then the top players could commit to every [competition]. Having it every year, it's just impossible to do that. That's the situation for the second round; that's the main reason why all the guys decided not to do it."

What a strange follow-up to the wonderful 1995 final. But it fits Sampras' pattern started in 1991. Disappointment and success go back and forth for him, in Davis Cup, as does his feeling for the competition when weighed against the prospect of major titles and major dollars.

"If I could be guaranteed a week off before and after the Davis Cup, I wouldn't have a problem committing," he said. "That means you have enough time to rest and recuperate. I don't see that happening."

Still, the price paid for 1995's success was worth it, Sampras said.

"Absolutely. The way it ended and to play the way I did the last couple of matches will bring back a lot of good memories for me and Davis Cup. I didn't start my career in Davis Cup all that great.

"But playing like I did [in Moscow]... maybe that can change some people's minds about me."

Davis Cup Record: Pete Sampras

Pete Sampras' Davis Cup reputation has come full circle, from a disappointing performance in his 1991 debut against France, to three days of clutch tennis against Russia in the 1995 final.

Davis Cup Record

Singles

1991 Final: France defeated United States 3–1

Opponent	Result	Score
Henri Leconte	L	6-4, 7-5, 6-4
Guy Forget	L	7-6, 3-6, 6-3, 6-4

1992 First round: United States defeated Argentina 5–0

Opponent	Result	Score
Martin Jaite	W	3-6, 6-4, 6-2, 6-4
Alberto Mancini	W	6-4, 6-1

1992 Quarter-finals: United States defeated Czechoslovakia 3–2

Opponent	Result	Score
Karel Novacek	W	6-3, 6-4, 6-2
Petr Korda	L	6-4, 6-3, 2-6, 6-3

1994 Quarter-finals: United States defeated The Netherlands 3–2

Opponent	Result	Score
Jacco Eltingh	W	6-2, 6-2, 6-0
Richard Krajicek	L	2-6, 7-5, 7-6, 7-5

1994 Semi-finals: Sweden defeated United States 3–2

Opponent	Result	Score
Magnus Larsson	W	6-7, 6-4, 6-2, 7-6
Stefan Edberg	L	6-3, retired (injury)

1995 Quarter-finals: United States defeated Italy 5–0

Opponent	Result	Score
Renzo Furlan	W	7-6, 6-3, 6-0
Andrea Gaudenzi	W	6-3, 1-6, 6-3

DAVIS CUP RECORD

1995 Semi-finals: United States defeated Sweden 4-1

Opponent	Result	Score
Thomas Enqvist	W	6-3, 6-4, 3-6, 6-3
Mats Wilander	W	2-6, 7-6, 6-3

1995 Final: United States defeated Russia 3-2

Opponent	Result	Score
Andrei Chesnokov	W	3-6, 6-4, 6-3, 6-7, 6-4
Yevgeny Kafelnikov	W	6-2, 6-4, 7-6

Doubles

1992 Semi-finals: United States defeated Sweden 4-1

Partner	Opponents	Result	Score
John McEnroe	Anders Jarryd		
	Stefan Edberg	W	6-1, 6-7, 4-6, 6-3, 6-3

1992 Final: United States defeated Switzerland 3-1

Partner	Opponents	Result	Score
John McEnroe	Marc Rosset		
	Jakob Hlasek	W	6-7, 6-7, 7-5, 6-1, 6-2

1995 Final: United States defeated Russia 3-2

Partner	Opponents	Result	Score
Todd Martin	Yevgeny Kafelnikov		
	Andrei Olhovskiy	W	7-5, 6-4, 6-3

Part III
Australian Open

Under The Weather Down Under 9

I T WAS cold. And windy. And rainy, a nasty sort of half-drizzle that doesn't soak you but rather sprays you, while chilling you to the bone.

Central Florida in January gets like that, the area's version of dead-of-winter. It's not snow, but it's not good, especially if it's the first blast of such weather.

It's midday in mid-January 1996 at Saddlebrook Resort in Wesley Chapel, site of the heralded Harry Hopman Tennis Academy that mainly caters to world-class junior players but has several top world tour professionals who periodically train or practise there.

Pete Sampras is the most famous of those. He likes Saddlebrook. It's a 20-minute dash north on Interstate 75 from his North Tampa home, 15 if he gets the urge to push his new Porsche Carrera, which he is known to do.

The Porsche is the main topic of conversation today, along with a trimmed-down Jennifer Capriati who plays on a nearby court. Capriati lives on the resort property, and for all the knocks against her intelligence, she's one of the smartest people around on this da She's out there moving around.

Sampras, in contrast, has cut a practice session short. The weather has worsened since early morning, and Sampras, who has been battling a nagging 'flu bug since Christmas, doesn't feel like fighting the wind, too. So he's standing there, talking about lunch, about the weather, about his Porsche that Hopman director Tommy Thompson just drove 120mph on some secluded country roads nearby, out of the reach of radar and redneck cops. He and Thompson exchange high-fives, laughing uproariously. Then Sampras coughs a couple of times, and there are some quick comments about the weather and the fact that he's standing there in shorts and sweatshirt, basically freezing to death.

This seems awfully casual behaviour for the world's No.1 player. During the Christmas holidays, he actually spent several days in bed with a fever. Now he was outside, being transformed into a human snow-cone, just asking for it.

No surprise, then, that when he went to Australia several days later the 'flu had worsened, the fever returned, and he found himself in a terrible way considering that the year's first Grand Slam, the Australian Open, was approaching.

The bug — which forced him to withdraw from an Open tune-up tournament — could be traced to December, a month when Sampras simply overdid it. Just a week after the Davis Cup final, the Grand Slam Cup was held in Munich, paying obscene amounts of money. Sampras reached the quarters, then returned home to Tampa, exhausted.

During a conversation over lunch that wind-chilled day, Sampras didn't seem himself. He didn't appear all that motivated at the prospect of winning an eighth Grand Slam title. He was sick and tired.

And good friend Tim Gullikson was sicker and surely more tired. His cancer continuing to worsen, Gullikson was in another round of treatments that could well be the last stand.

So it was a subdued Sampras who flew a full day to Australia.

The idea of him reaching a third consecutive Open final was far-fetched, considering his state of mind — and body.

Sampras arrived in Melbourne on a Wednesday, five days before the Open began. He went straight from the airport to Flinders Park, site of the Australian National Tennis Center, to practise with fellow American Aaron Krickstein.

Sampras stepped off the plane and encountered the sort of heat he's used to in Tampa — in July. No wonder he practised only half an hour. He had to stop several times because of a nosebleed, brought on by the cabin's dry air during his flight.

"I'm fading," Sampras said toward the end of the hit.

Not a pretty picture, nor a championship one. But even if he looked bad or lost early, Sampras was going to compete.

"I was going to play this tournament no matter what, unless I was on my deathbed," Sampras said after the workout. "I'm still a little congested but it shouldn't give me a problem. I'm just a little tired from the flight, but I feel fine."

He couldn't have felt good about his draw, though: Australian Richard Fromberg in the first round, up-and-coming American Mike Joyce in the second round, then, once again, Mark Philippoussis.

A possible rematch with Philippoussis was immediately viewed as a land mine for an ill-prepared Sampras. Philippoussis was starting to harness his weaponry under the guidance of new coach Nick Bollettieri.

"Pete sometimes can be vulnerable the first week," said Brad Gilbert, Agassi's coach. "Pete's been a little sick and hasn't played that much. I look for him to have some tougher matches [early] than Andre, but once he gets through the first week of a tournament he's a different player."

Australia's National Sports Book installed Sampras as the tournament favourite, at 5-4. Agassi followed at 3-1.

Philippoussis was 100-1.

Natural Affinity 10

WHERE does the Australian Open fit in, in the Sampras Grand Slam ranking order? Alas, it must be fourth. That flies in the face of the natural affinity he has for the event, given his feeling for the old Aussies, their accomplishments and their attitudes. Such a revelation — though it is hardly that considering the status of the other three Grand Slams — will disappoint the legion of Sampras fans in Melbourne, which has a large Greek community and has always claimed the half-Greek Sampras as one of its own.

On a simpler, totally unromantic scale, Sampras loves the event because it's hassle-free. Sampras detests hassles. During tournaments, particularly Grand Slam tournaments, he likes to be comfortable, with good room service and television as absolute musts. He also likes easy access to the site. That's where the Australian Open scores big.

"As far as the majors go, the Australian is the most convenient," Sampras said. "The hotel where the players stay is five minutes from the courts."

Convenience. That puts it all in perspective right there. But in truth, that convenience is part of the overall modernisation of the Australian Open that has enabled it, finally, to take its appropriate place in the Grand Slam line-up. Begun in 1905, the tournament was played on grass, at three different sites, until 1988 when the National Tennis Center opened with its Rebound Ace hard courts and a retractable roof over the main court. Full-fledged fields have followed, distancing the Open from its history of inconsistent draws. For years, those draws were Aussie-dominated, due to the continent's isolation from the rest of the globe. Then came a period when the January trip, landing one smack in the middle of the blazing Australian summer, was too much for many players.

It bottomed out from 1978-80. Borg, McEnroe, Connors and others were absent those years, allowing the Argentinian clay-court grinder Guillermo Vilas, seldom a factor on grass with his big looping top spin groundstrokes, to win back to back in 1978-79, defeating John Marks the first year, John Sadri the second. In 1980, American Brian Teacher defeated Kim Warwick in yet another forgettable final.

Same deal on the women's side. In 1978 the legendary Chris O'Neil defeated Betsy Nagelsen for the title. In 1979, doubles specialist Barbara Jordan beat Sharon Walsh in the final. Martina Navratilova wasn't entered; neither was Chris Evert, Tracy Austin or Billie Jean King.

Sampras himself has passed on the tournament twice due to injuries, in 1991-92, after playing the two years before that with mixed results — a first-round loss in 1989, a fourth-round advancement in 1990, the latter effort a preview of what would come in September at the US Open.

Sampras started the 1990 Australian with a five-set victory over compatriot Tim Mayotte, 12-10 in the fifth. It was one of the longer matches in tournament history at 70 games but nowhere near the longest. That was 94 games, when Dennis Ralston beat John Newcombe in the 1970 quarters, before tie-breakers, with 19-17 and 20-18 sets.

Another five-set victory, this one over Jordi Arrese, was also significant in that Sampras dropped the first set 6-0. A third-round victory over Aussie Todd Woodbridge came in straight sets, despite a pro-Woody crowd. And there was no dishonour in going down to Yannick Noah in the fourth round; Noah, in his next-to-last year on the world tour, was making his final run at a Grand Slam title, ultimately reaching the semi-finals.

After the two-year break, in 1993 Sampras returned to Melbourne and got his all-out quest for the No.1 world ranking off-and-rolling. He reached the semi-finals where he faced Edberg for the seventh time; after losing to the Swede in the previous year's US Open final, Sampras prevailed in the ATP Championships to even the head-to-head mark at 3-3. This time, Edberg was all over Sampras, winning in three sets en route to a second consecutive final against Jim Courier. As in 1992, Courier defeated Edberg for the title.

But Sampras was clearly on his way. In three months he would supplant Courier as world No.1. By the time Sampras returned to Flinders Park, he had a stranglehold on the spot.

Sampras came to Australia in 1994 having won the last two Grand Slams, Wimbledon and the US Open. He won a total of eight tournaments in 1993, building a huge lead in the ATP Tour rankings. And with three Grand Slam titles at the age of 22, the first comparisons to the all-time greats were cropping up.

The comparisons were rampant after the 1994 final, in which Sampras defeated Todd Martin in straight sets. It was a final that was reminiscent of the old days: serve-and-volleyers who said not a word, letting their tennis talk for them. Both players have been repeatedly bashed as boring, albeit effective. Neither lets such criticism affect them on court.

"It makes it more fun for me when people appreciate two guys who just go out and play tennis," Sampras said. "I think that's the way tennis should be played — with class, without losing your temper or embarrassing yourself."

Sampras, in taking a fourth Grand Slam championship, became the first man to win Wimbledon, the US Open and the Australian Open consecutively since Roy Emerson in 1964-65.

A Human Touch 11

JANUARY 1995: Something was terribly wrong with Tim
Gullikson. Late in 1994, he had started to show the first signs
of illness. In October, there was an inexplicable collapse in a
Stockholm hotel room. Gullikson fell into a glass table, breaking
his nose, the shattered glass cutting ugly gashes in his face. Before
passing out, he was on the phone with Agassi's coach, Brad
Gilbert, who answered the telephone at the Stockholm Open's
practice courts. He couldn't make out what Gilbert was saying.
Gilbert couldn't understand him.

Two months later, in Munich, after doctors back home in
Wheaton, Illinois, said Gullikson had a faulty heart valve, he was
on the phone again, this time with his wife Rosemary, when his
speech once more became garbled. He spent the next week in a
hospital, where he was told he had suffered two strokes, and that,
yes, he had some heart trouble.

The 1995 season began, and he and Sampras took off to Australia, continuing their quest for Grand Slam championships. A
season seemingly full of promise, Sampras eager to leave behind
the late-summer 1994 failure at the US Open and Davis Cup, bent
on retaining the No.1 world ranking that Agassi was closing in on.
Gullikson also was on the run.

January 20, following a workout with Sampras before a third-round Australian Open match, Gullikson could run no more. He passed out, was taken to another hospital, this time in Melbourne, and got another faulty diagnosis: melanoma. In the brain. Six months to live, at most.

Unfortunately, this diagnosis was closer to the truth. Something, indeed, was terribly wrong.

Gullikson flew back home, where doctors finally got it right. His brain was being ravaged by a rare cancer, oligodendroglioma.

The silver lining: it was treatable.

Before the latest, correct diagnosis came down, Sampras heard the first, bludgeoning verdict.

He then went about trying to win a major tennis tournament.

Sampras played splendidly in a third-round victory over Lars Jonsson, losing only seven games before dashing to the hospital. In the fourth round against another, much more capable Swede, Magnus Larsson, the strain showed. Sampras dropped the first two sets before serving himself out of trouble, to the second victory of his career from a 0-2 set deficit.

Gullikson had flown back home, Sampras feared, to die. So there you have the mindset of the world's No.1 player as he approached what promised to be another dogfight against Courier, in the Open's quarter-finals.

Sampras had spent much of his off-court time at the hospital with Tim Gullikson and his brother Tom, feeling the helplessness of watching a friend faced with the ultimate finality.

He took that helplessness to the court, and ended up sharing it with the 15,000 centre court spectators and countless more back home who watched on ESPN.

The drama developed slowly. Matches between Sampras and Courier are so steeped in slugging that the nuances, the slight differences that tilt a match one way or another, can be overlooked.

Courier — who was playing some of his best tennis in years that January, with a tournament title and an eight-match (all straight sets) victory streak — took the first two sets, tie-breakers both. Sampras came back to take the next two.

As Sampras walked back to serve the fifth set's opening game, a spectator called out to him, unaware that he would reach not only the player's ears, but his heart and soul as well.

"Do it for your coach," the fan implored.

It was a simple, direct plea. The sort of thing Sampras might yell if he were a fan. To the point. Effective.

Sampras held to start the set, and sought the brief refuge of the changeover. Reaching for a towel, it began. Sampras buried his face, weeping. Then, a splash of cold water and he was up, his extremely private side bared like never before for the public.

Courier held for 1-1, shifting the pressure back to Sampras. At 30-0, after a 118-mph ace, his emotions overcame him at an immeasurable speed. Sampras, the man who had been labelled the world over as a free-swinging, non-feeling, modern-day tennis robot, stood at the baseline, rigid almost, with tears streaming down his five o'clock shadowy visage.

Then came two more promptings. One, softly, from the side; Sampras' girlfriend Delaina Mulcahy saying, "Come on, honey, get in there." Another, from across the net; Courier calling out, "Are you all right, Pete? You know, we can do this tomorrow if you want."

Mulcahy's words soothed Sampras. Courier's angered him, because, contrary to what was widely reported, Sampras thought his old chum was being slightly sarcastic, even though Courier was aware of Gullikson's health.

"I thought he was giving me some shit," Sampras said.

Prompted by both urgings, Sampras aced Courier through the tears, his 20th ace of the match, then held with a service winner. Courier then began to cramp, and when he was broken in the seventh game, he was done. Sampras served out the match with his 23rd ace and yet another service winner.

It was 1:09am in Australia.

Match of the year. Here it was late January, and that honour already was being thrust upon the quarter-final. Sampras got an ovation from the media when he walked into the interview room, the no-cheering-by-journalists dictum discarded. That brought him to tears again, and he left, returning a bit later.

"Win or lose, I thought it was one of the better matches I've ever taken part in," Sampras said. "I just didn't quit."

Delaina at courtside. That was a nice touch. During the Sampras-Courier quarter-final, EPSN reporter Mary Carillo scored big, reaching Mulcahy, who told the world that Sampras was "so emotionally exhausted from this whole thing. He wants to do it for Tim."

It was a rare media moment for Mulcahy, who has largely remained in the background since becoming Sampras' first true love almost overnight in 1990. She has endured the older-woman talk — she's only six years older than Sampras. She has endured the gold-digging gossip that says she targeted Sampras for his money. Depending on whom you talk to, on a given day at a professional tournament, opinions of her can range widely. The fact that she used to be the girlfriend of Sampras' former agent, Gavin Forbes, doesn't help.

But such talk comes with celebrity. Always, there is someone, somewhere disbelieving that Mulcahy and Sampras could simply meet, fall in love and stay together. Too easy. Too '50s. Those people have never seen Sampras' sheepish, goofy, toothy grin when asked a question about Mulcahy that's even remotely personal.

Their first date, at Sampras' invitation, lasted a week, at a resort in Myrtle Beach, South Carolina. Their first house, on Sampras' tab, is a $770,000, 7,865-square-foot pad in an exclusive development called Tampa Palms. Sampras lives in a section called The Reserve, next door to another millionaire athlete, Tampa Bay Bucanneers quarterback Trent Dilfer. Sampras, Mulcahy and their two weimaraners share the home, purchased in December 1992.

It's a spacious place, with a patio/pool area of almost 2,000 square feet, and a designer-brick driveway that cost more than many people's cars. It's a place Sampras plans on staying for at least a few more years.

Early in 1996, while playing a tournament in San Jose, he talked to the media about one day returning to California to be near his family and his roots. A story developed that he soon would leave Tampa. One close Tampa friend more or less confirmed that, saying, "He'll leave eventually; he'll get a better deal somewhere else."

Sampras is in no hurry. "I've spent a lot of money on my house," he said. "Done a lot to it. It's a nice house."

Some would say Mulcahy has spent the money.

But others would say better she than Sampras.

There was a slight hint of frugality seen in a promotional video released by Nike in 1995, shot in Sampras' home. He jokingly opened his pantry for the camera. Inside were canned foods. Generic brands.

On the other hand, when he opened the refrigerator, there sat a six-pack of Heineken. And Sampras doesn't drink. Delaina, that spendthrift.

Mulcahy recently finished law school at Stetson University, in nearby St Petersburg, Florida, an accomplishment that, given her age and the man she lives with, can't be overlooked.

"Delaina seems very intrigued about finding her own place in the world, and I've always admired that," said journalist Sandra Harwitt. "I know a lot of people thought she was just 'moving up' by getting together with Pete. I never thought that.

"I also think it's a great sign of who Pete 'is,' how good a person he is, that he wants her to have something on her own. They're very much a couple. A lot of pro tennis players have had everything focused toward them, from the time they were little kids. But I think this relationship shows a rather unselfish quality in Pete."

"I don't feel any sort of guilt [about my lifestyle] because she's in law school," Sampras said. "I've always told her she's got to do what she wants to do and not be dependent on me. She needs to have her own career and her own goals and not live vicariously through my life. I think it's really great for our relationship that she has her own agenda. That's really important."

As for the two marrying... hard to say. Early in 1995, pressed with some personal questions by Australian *Tennis* magazine writer Paul Fein, Sampras conceded that he is deeply in love with Mulcahy, but added that there were no plans in the near future for us to get married. There's no rush really for me. We rarely talk about it."

Some people close to the couple tell another story, about how Mulcahy has repeatedly suggested marriage, with Sampras balking each and every time.

Some even that suggest Sampras should get his palimony plans in order — now.

But what about the way Sampras' eyes go wide when talking about his companion? Mulcahy, after all, is a beautiful woman. Just as Sampras could find someone else if he had the opportunity, so, surely, could she.

They do, as Harwitt said, seem like a true couple. And if you believe a January 1996 report by *The Sunday Mirror, a* London tabloid, an especially amorous couple.

The Mirror, somehow, came up with photos of Mulcahy — at least, they look like Mulcahy — in sexy, black lingerie. The pictures may have been the real thing, but the story accompanying them got too weird. It reported that the photos had love notes from Mulcahy to Sampras attached, but were found in Andre Agassi's hotel room in Philadelphia, possibly part of a joke that backfired.

The story's headline: 'At your service, Pete.'

These people — this *couple* — then, seem to deserve their due, if for nothing else, because together they bring an aspect to Sampras' existence that races light years beyond his public image as a walking cure for insomnia.

Pete Sampras boring? A poll, please: Since when is an impetuous first date that involves travel to a resort and lasts a week indicative of a dull bachelor?

Word on the circuit is that Sampras may well have been a virgin before meeting Mulcahy or, at best, a novice in life's real game of singles. The fact that he found the courage even to approach Mulcahy, much less ask her out, *much* less fall into a full-fledged affair almost from the outset, shows a part of Sampras that rarely surfaces. This move, for a 19-year-old, took as much nerve, or more, than serving for the match in a Grand Slam final.

And what about those tabloid pictures? One wants to believe they're the real thing because they strongly indicate that Sampras, with much help from his mate, is the real thing and not just another overgrown tennis tyke sitting around thinking *only* about Laver and his next gargantuan paycheck.

Look at those pictures, and you want to grab Sampras, slap him silly and tell him he better *not* be sitting around thinking only about tennis. Because, given life's twists and turns, the tennis could be gone tomorrow. And it could be wonderful if and when that happens, that he had Delaina Mulcahy to come home to.

Likewise, Mulcahy could do a lot worse than a clean-living, idealistic-driven athlete like Sampras.

All this makes for good copy, of course, and gossipy — albeit harmless — debate among Sampras' fans who take their support to a more personal level.

They've debated on the Internet. America Online's computer service features an extensive tennis section, with various 'message boards' through which fans can spout and exchange views on different tennis-related subjects. The Pete Sampras message board is extremely popular, right up there with two others — Monica Seles and gay and lesbian tennis issues.

The Sampras-Mulcahy relationship has lit up the board more than a few times. Here are some random selections from some of 1996's postings, supplied without AOL identifications, of course:

Q: "Nice lady, cradle-robber or gold-digger?"

A: "Seems as though the jury is still out on that one."

From an obviously younger female fan: "I LOVE Pete Sampras. I'm going to have to do something about his girlfriend, since Pete and I are ultimately going to fall in love and get married."

And finally, some perspective, via one of the longer postings:

"Although their relationship is unusual because of the age difference, Delaina obviously adores Pete and seems to have been instrumental — along with Tim Gullikson, of course — in Pete's success over the last few years."

The relationship also has been tested by the ongoing female adulation Sampras encounters on the road. Okay, so it's not like Agassi's situation. There are no stories of Sampras spending any nights with porno stars, as Agassi was alleged to have done early in 1996, right before he and Brooke Shields announced engagement plans. Still, though, there is a certain sexuality between Sampras and his female fans. Sampras is a sleeper in this competition, a dark horse. But he is a contender.

"Pete must love [Delaina], because he could be screwing everything if he wanted to right now," said one former top player.

Sampras seems uncomfortable when confronted with even a hint of that reality.

In the fall of 1995, Sampras volunteered to play tennis against a variety of well-heeled hackers to raise money for a mental health facility in Tampa. Things were going well, when the event was cut short by rain. Sampras and 30 to 40 people scampered into the organiser's home — the tennis was played on the organiser's private court. Sampras then went about signing autographs for an hour. For most of that hour, a woman in her mid-30s stood next to the table where Sampras was signing. She didn't say much. Just stared. And smiled. Almost drooling, really.

When she finally walked away, someone mentioned to Sampras that she had been checking him out. He acted incredulous.

Sampras gets the younger ones excited, too. Evonne Goolagong, the former great player, has a 19-year-old daughter, Kelly. Goolagong likes to show off her picture and watch people's jaws drop. Kelly is a knockout. Kelly, her mom says, is "wild about Pete."

When Sampras heard that story, he laughed. "Really?" he asked. Nothing else. No locker-room reaction. Not much of a reaction, period, other than a big smile. Of course, he hadn't seen the picture.

Sampras goes out of his way to downplay even a suggestion of impropriety. Last year there was a rumour that he was seen on the road in the company of a sultry blonde, when Mulcahy was back home in Tampa. If you hadn't heard the rumour, Sampras made sure you had — so he could deny it, fervently.

Delaina aside, Sampras was truly alone when the Gulliksons flew back to the US. As remarkable as his survivals against Larsson and Courier were, his semi-final victory over Chang stands on its own merit. Cumulatively, Sampras had gone through the toughest ten days of his career to reach this stage.

After taking three more hours to beat Chang in four sets, Sampras acknowledged that fact. In the process, he said, that had made it something special, setting it apart even from his five previous major title runs.

"That's because of the circumstances and the fact that I was down and out against Larsson and down and out against Courier," Sampras said. "I really fought back and showed more heart this week than I probably ever have, just refusing to go down without a fight. That's really important to me because I think I've shown a lot of people that I might look kind of lackadaisical, but deep down inside I'm doing whatever I can to try and win."

Sampras seemed put off slightly by the public's reaction to his 'human side'. It bothered him that it took such a drastic show of emotion to, finally, start winning people over.

"I think people understand that I'm normal, that I have feelings like everyone else, that I'm not a robot out there; that I play the way I play and the way I carry myself is just the way I am. I'm as normal as anyone else. [Tim's illness] was a very tough thing to go through."

On the other half of the draw, Agassi was brandishing his new short-hair/bandana look while building on his US Open momentum. Agassi loves hard-court tennis, where he can time his short hop perfectly, just like Connors did, and bash the ball from side to side. And now that Gilbert had him thinking, too, the package was complete.

The final showcased the budding Sampras-Agassi rivalry, and it went Agassi's way because of a third set tie-breaker in which Sampras showed another human quality: the ability to let a sure thing slip away.

After a split of the first two sets, Sampras led the tie-breaker 6-4. With the set on his racquet, Sampras could only wave at an Agassi forehand return: 6-5. Agassi served and rallied patiently — thoughtfully — until he coaxed a Sampras error.

With two set points saved, Agassi raced home, first with a service winner, then a bodacious backhand drop volley that capped a 13-stroke trade.

The last set went routinely. Agassi wrapped up a 4-6, 6-1, 7-6 (8-6), 6-4 against a player who, finally, gave out.

"I have to say what I witnessed Pete do in the past two weeks, with the difficulties about his coach, is absolutely inspiring," Agassi said. "His courage on and off the court... we can all learn from what he did."

The crowd saw Sampras break down again, in a short post-match speech. "I just want to let Tim know I keep thinking about him and that I wish he was here," Sampras said.

There was danger in overlooking the tennis, so fraught with emotion was the final. Sampras had 28 aces. Agassi made only 26 unforced errors, a Gilbert-constructed statistic most certainly.

"I'm not going to out-rally Andre," Sampras said. "He's probably one of the best guys in the world in ground-stroke confrontations. I need to come in, go for winners, mix it up.

"If Andre stays fit, he's a threat to win every major tournament of the year. Tennis has been missing a rivalry. Andre and I could be a great one. Our games are very different and we are very different. If we're playing in Grand Slams that's great for the game. Andre is a guy who puts tennis on the front pages of sports pages. Tennis needs that."

Scudded 12

SAMPRAS carried the emotional baggage of 1995 with him to Australia in 1996. He didn't want to admit that. Such a concession would lay groundwork for excuses if things didn't go right. Sampras doesn't make excuses. He wanted to present a calm, controlled front impervious to the effects of remembrance.

"It will bring back a lot of memories," he said prior to leaving, "but it's not going to feel any different [at the tournament]. It's been a year now."

Sampras' cold subsided slightly as the tournament approached, possibly helped by the heat. In beating Richard Fromberg in the first round, in straight sets, he looked healthy, but rusty. His serve faltered enough to allow Fromberg ten break points. Not one was cashed in.

"The first round of a major is always a tough match to get through," Sampras said. "I went in not really sure how my form was going to be. Under the circumstances I thought I hit the ball pretty well. I just didn't serve great. Hopefully my tennis can get better as the week goes on."

It did in the second round, in a four-set victory over Joyce. Twenty aces were key.

"To serve that many aces just gives me a better opportunity to hold on to my serve," he said.

"My serve was a lot better than in the first match [against

Fromberg]. I didn't hit the ball as well [overall] but my serve was just on."

Serving well — serving *aces* — led immediately to a dialogue regarding the next match, against Philippoussis. Sampras talked about the need to be consistent. To hear one of tennis' ultimate power players worry about getting the ball in court says a lot about Philippoussis.

"He's dangerous, one of the most dangerous guys we have on the tour," Sampras said.

"He has a big serve and backs it up with some good groundies. That was a dangerous match at the US Open. After losing the first set I kind of scrapped and clawed my way back to end up winning. My plan against him is just to get the ball back and make him play as much as possible and just go from there.

"Mark's got the weapons and that's the first thing I look at in a young guy coming up, to see if he has the weapons. I was pretty impressed when we played in [New York]. If I can get him moving, that's great. I want to be the guy at the net trying to dictate play as much as I can because if I don't he's going to want to take charge."

There also was the hometown factor to consider. Sampras couldn't even count on Melbourne's Greeks this time. Philippoussis is one of them.

"It was tough [enough] playing him at the US Open," Sampras said. "I'm sure he'll have his fans, but I've been in this type of situation before. Hopefully I'll get through it. I try to get off to a good start [in these situations] and try to take the crowd out of the match. I don't think it's going to be like a Davis Cup match but certainly he'll be the crowd favourite."

Philippoussis said he would cope with the moment by trying "to not think about playing Sampras. I won't worry about the outcome. It might be a great atmosphere out there so I will just enjoy myself."

Here's a kicker: The match ended up being played indoors, technically. The retractable roof on centre court was closed earlier in the day due to rain. It stayed closed, keeping the damp air out, making Philippoussis' serves even tougher.

He aced Sampras 29 times. He mashed forehands into the corners. Sampras was gone in three sets: 6-4, 7-6 (11-9), 7-6 (6-3).

So was his No.1 world ranking. Andre Agassi, by making the semi-finals, assumed the position, albeit briefly. Thomas Muster reached No.1 in early February and set off a six-month debate over the validity of the ATP Tour rankings.

There was no debate about what transpired between Sampras and Philippoussis.

"He was just on today, plain and simple," Sampras said. "The one thing I was pretty concerned about going into the match was if he was on and there was no question he was at the top of his game. I was surprised he was able to maintain that level for the three sets, you know; I really didn't have a sniff at getting his serve back."

Not completely accurate. Sampras got a look at two break points, one in each of the first two sets. In the third set, Sampras — who had his own service broken but once the entire match — won only five points when Philippoussis served.

Philippoussis said he had ventured into tennis nirvana, that netherworld known as 'the zone'.

"I felt like I could toss the ball up and ace however I wanted to," Philippoussis said. "It was an unbelievable feeling. I mean, I've felt it before, but I just felt I could do no wrong on the serve.

"The good thing is I concentrated really well for the whole match. I thought maybe I would lose my concentration, maybe in the third set, when I had a few break points and didn't take them. But it was surprising; it's as if as the match went on I got better and better."

Philippoussis benefited from the US Open experience when he gave himself little chance of winning, aiming instead to merely play well.

"It was my first time in the third round of a Grand Slam tournament and I was playing Pete Sampras on a huge centre court," he said. "At first I just wanted to get out there and have fun. [This time] I gave myself a chance because there's no point walking out there if you haven't got a chance to win. I just wanted to forget who he was and just think of him as another player."

Easier said than done.

"I look up to Pete very much," Philippoussis said. "Also Boris Becker, just because of the way they handle themselves on the court. Pete is very calm and if he does get pumped up, I'm sure he gets pumped up on the inside, he doesn't show it much."

"I watched the second and third sets," Agassi said, "and I felt like, for a third-round match, I've seen Pete play at that level and beat a lot of guys. But it was definitely one of those draws where he was going to have to play at 85 per cent instead of 70 per cent. He was at his 70 per cent, but the fact that he lost his serve only one time the whole match says a lot for how he competed.

"But... it just seemed like Philippoussis didn't miss a whole lot, and I'm sure Pete was counting on some of that."

"It's obvious he's very talented," Sampras said. "Time will tell if he can be consistent. When I played him at the US Open he had his ups and downs that I was able to take advantage of. This time he didn't give me those opportunities. His first-serve percentage seemed like 90 per cent. I didn't play bad. It's just that when he's serving that big there's really nothing you can do."

It sounded like Agassi, talking about Sampras, after the 1990 and 1995 US Open finals.

The setting of the upset precipitated comparisons between Philippoussis and Sampras, past their eyebrows and their serves. People recalled Sampras when he was 19, winning that first Open title, and saw a second coming.

"We're both Greek," Sampras said, "and that's similar. We both serve well and go for our shots. I was still pretty green at that point and so is he, but he's got the game and the strength to kind of overwhelm you."

"I suppose I do look up to Pete, also, because he had a Greek background," Philippoussis said.

Comparisons stopped two days later. Philippoussis lost in the fourth round to fellow Aussie Mark Woodforde.

So much for the second coming.

Sampras hadn't lost a Grand Slam tournament match in straight sets since the 1993 Australian semi-finals, to Stefan Edberg. Then, and now, he was coming off an all-too-brief respite after an emotional, successful Davis Cup final.

Two months after the Australian, at the Lipton Championships, Sampras was forced to defend his decision to skip the first two Davis Cup competitions.

Exhibit A: Mark Philippoussis.

"After the Russian experience I was physically injured and mentally — I didn't want to pick up a racquet for a couple of weeks; I didn't really want to do a lot of training after that," he said, in a most telling revelation. Sampras has been known to get antsy after only a couple of days off, missing the sound of the gut whacking the ball.

"I went down to Australia pretty unprepared. I think my tennis probably spoke for itself.

"The one thing I want to do is give myself the best chance I can at the major tournaments. I don't know if the Davis Cup final took a lot out of me or what, but I certainly didn't feel ready to go."

Despite that, Sampras certainly wasn't ready to give up his No.1 ranking. All along he had trotted out the cliché that "you don't own the No.1 spot, you just rent it," but Sampras felt deep down that he had a lease that had been prematurely voided.

"What's more important is to be No.1 at the end of the year. This is not a great start [to 1996] but there's a lot of tennis to be played. I just have to get over this loss and try to have a good next couple of months. The French Open is coming up... and I'm looking forward to that. It'll take a little time to get over this but I've lost before and I'll have to bounce back. Hopefully I can regain that No.1 ranking."

Losing it to Agassi didn't bother Sampras as much as the

inevitable takeover by Muster, a man who, if all tournaments were played on hard courts would struggle to make the top 20. Muster is a living, breathing example of why the ATP Tour's 'best of 14' ranking system isn't valid. By allowing a player to count only his best 14 tournament finishes, it enables a one-dimensional performer like Muster to construct a cache of points on the surface of his choice. Muster became No.1 even though he had played Wimbledon only four times. With a record of 0-4, it should be noted — and abhorred. Winless — and sometimes absent — at Wimbledon, yet the world's top-ranked player. If that isn't oil and water, what is?

When the debate ensued, Agassi, the immediately deposed, quickly became the most outspoken critic of Muster's rise, taking plenty of time to laud Sampras as the only rightful No.1 — other than himself, of course. But this was a time to appreciate Agassi. Sampras wasn't going to speak up as loudly. And really, Sampras' voice wasn't going to be listened to as extensively as Agassi, the game's one, true star who transcends tennis in the public consciousness.

"It's not for me to say that I'm better than Muster or that Pete's better than Muster," said Agassi. "I just know that when I step on the court I would fear playing Pete 99.9 per cent of the time more than Muster. That shouldn't be a shock to anybody; Pete's been on the top of the game for three years.

"I've always had complaints about the ranking system, but you can't take away the work that Thomas has put into it."

This was Agassi in January. As the season moved into spring, his words would have a harsher bite, and Muster would respond, at one point saying he had earned the ranking because he had earned the points. "You don't buy the points in a supermarket," Muster said.

Sampras weighed in occasionally, and for the sake of impact that was a good thing. Less meant more. The idea of Sampras speaking out about anything is fairly shocking when it comes right down to it. But on the Muster/No.1 issue Sampras came off as thoughtful, a tour spokesman almost, at the age of 24.

"I feel that Muster is the best player in the world on clay," Sampras said in March 1996. "As far as him being the best player on anything but clay, I don't swallow that quite as well. He had a phenomenal [1995], winning the French Open and ten other clay-court tournaments, and the way the ranking system is with defending points [earned from the previous year] he just kind of snuck up and became No.1.

"But I've said this before. It really just comes down to the end of the year. That is when you add and subtract all of your points and you will have your final ranking. And *that* is the true indication of who the best player in the world is. If Thomas would be No.1 at the end of the year that would mean a lot more to me personally — and to the game — versus, you know, being No.1 in March of whatever. [The end of the year] is a true indication of who had the most consistent year. The ranking system... all I can say is that you're not going to find a perfect system that everyone is happy with, and the only problem I have with the system is that I feel like every time you walk out on the court it should count, and that's not the case right now."

Australian Open Record: Pete Sampras

Pete Sampras loves the Australian Open's tradition, its hard-court surface and its first-rate facilities. No wonder he has won the tournament twice and finished second another time.

Australian Open Record

1989

First round	Lost to Christian Saceanu	6-4, 6-4, 7-6

1990

First round	Defeated Tim Mayotte	7-6, 6-7, 4-6, 7-5, 12-10
Second round	Defeated Jordi Arrese	0-6, 6-2, 3-6, 6-1, 6-3
Third round	Defeated Todd Woodbridge	7-5, 6-4, 6-2
Fourth round	Lost to Yannick Noah	6-3, 6-4, 3-6, 6-2

1991

Did not play

1992

Did not play

1993

First round	Defeated Carl-Uwe Steeb	6-1, 6-2, 6-1
Second round	Defeated Magnus Larsson	6-3, 3-6, 6-3, 6-4
Third round	Defeated Alex Antonitsch	7-6, 6-4, 6-2
Fourth round	Defeated Mal Washington	6-3, 6-4, 6-4
Quarter-finals	Defeated Brett Steven	6-3, 6-2, 6-3
Semi-finals	Lost to Stefan Edberg	7-6, 6-3, 7-6

1994

First round	Defeated Josh Eagle	6-4, 6-0, 7-6
Second round	Defeated Yevgeny Kafelnikov	6-3, 2-6, 6-3, 1-6, 9-7
Third round	Defeated Stephane Simian	7-5, 6-1, 1-6, 6-4
Fourth round	Defeated Ivan Lendl	7-6, 6-2, 7-6
Quarter-finals	Defeated Magnus Gustafsson	7-6, 2-6, 6-3, 7-6
Semi-finals	Defeated Jim Courier	6-3, 6-4, 6-4
Final	Defeated Todd Martin	7-6, 6-4, 6-4

1995

First round	Defeated Gianlucca Pozzi	6-3, 6-2 ,6-0
Second round	Defeated Jan Kroslak	6-2, 6-0, 6-1
Third round	Defeated Lars Jonsson	6-1, 6-2, 6-4
Fourth round	Defeated Magnus Larsson	4-6, 6-7, 7-5, 6-4, 6-4
Quarter-finals	Defeated Jim Courier	6-7, 6-7, 6-3, 6-4, 6-3
Semi-finals	Defeated Michael Chang	6-7, 6-3, 6-4, 6-4
Final	Lost to Andre Agassi	4-6, 6-1, 7-6, 6-4

1996

First round	Defeated Richard Fromberg	7-5, 6-3, 6-2
Second round	Defeated Michael Joyce	3-6, 6-3, 6-4, 6-4
Third round	Lost to Mark Philippoussis	6-4, 7-6, 7-6

1997

First round	Defeated Dinu Pescariu	6-2, 6-4, 6-2
Second round	Defeated Adrian Voinea	3-6, 6-2, 6-3, 6-2
Third round	Defeated Mark Woodforde	6-1, 6-0, 6-1
Fourth round	Defeated Dominik Hrbaty	6-7, 6-3, 6-4, 3-6, 6-4
Quarter-finals	Defeated Alberto Costa	6-3, 6-7, 6-1, 3-6, 6-2
Semi-finals	Defeated Thomas Muster	6-1, 7-6, 6-3
Final	Defeated Carlos Moya	6-2, 6-3, 6-3

Career won-lost: 30-5

Part IV
French Open

"He Taught Me To Compete" 13

In the tie-break of your life
While friends and family, children and wife looked on
You fought right to the end
I always will remember you, my friend

You faced the ups and downs
At length in weakness found your greatest strength
Cheered by the prayers that all did send
So many will remember you, my friend

At match point came your victory
For through this veil of tears I see
That life's game we must lose to win
The cup of true remembrance, my friend

And so we're left to struggle on
The points seem harder, and so long
And injured hearts will slowly mend
healed by our memory of you, my friend

Gully's Song ('My Friend')★

Gully was gone.

On the afternoon of May 3, 1996, a Friday afternoon, Tim Gullikson, age 44, succumbed to the cancer that had consumed his life but not his spirit.

He left behind a wife, Rosemary.

Two young children, Erik and Megan.

A twin brother, Tom. A mother.

And Pete Sampras.

When this life and Tim Gullikson parted company, Sampras had been doing what his coach would have wanted. Practising. Trying to inch closer to solving his personal mystery of mastering clay-court tennis. Sampras toiled longer than usual that day at Saddlebrook. Mulcahy, starting a weekend that was supposed to be one of celebration — she was graduating from law school — took the call, heard the terrible, inevitable news first.

Sampras was preparing for the European challenge. In contrast to 1995 when he had gone over early and played several events before the French Open, he opted in 1996 for one tune-up, the Italian Open. A prudent choice. He won the tournament in 1994 and that had remained the highlight of his clay play until the 1995 Davis Cup final.

Sampras had carried on with his preparation in the face of Gullikson's worsening condition. In April, he had gone to visit his coach and was shocked at the deterioration. It had been a quick decline for Gullikson, the final plunge of the roller-coaster that had carried all his family and friends to a temporary summit the previous late summer and autumn, when he was responding favourably to treatments.

★ © 1996 by Bruce Wright

Gullikson's coaching-by-phone had lessened gradually, and Sampras had begun resigning himself to what was ahead. But he still wasn't ready for the shock, for the experience of Gullikson's funeral, in Wheaton, Illinois; Sampras had never even attended a funeral before. He served as a pallbearer and set his 1993 Wimbledon trophy next to the coffin as a final tribute to the man he told the funeral audience "taught me to compete — and how to win."

And so, initially he recoiled.

The morning after Gullikson's death he was back out at Saddlebrook. A tribute to his coach. But he was going through the motions, no more. After returning from the funeral he withdrew from the Italian and announced that he was considering missing the French, too. Wimbledon? A definite. But the grind of red-clay tennis was too much, too soon.

"I'm just not up to it," Sampras said.

Sampras came round in time for the French. Surely spurred by memory, or something else somewhat indefinable. In their brief time together, Sampras and Gullikson had become soulmates of a sort. For whatever reason, they had connected and discovered a shared destiny of travelling the globe in search of major championships, in search of history. But along the way their journey had taken on a deeper meaning.

"It's hard to have friends on the tour and I'm a very private person anyway," Sampras said after Gullikson fell ill. "When Tim's not around it's not just that I'm missing my coach. It's that I'm missing my best friend."

Maybe Sampras' soul was searching, when he reconsidered and started packing for Paris, tossing a necklace, with a charm given to him by to Gullikson for good luck, into his tennis bag. An inanimate object, it was a simple, glorious symbol of Sampras' feelings.

Just as symbolic was Sampras' decision to play the French. This would be his first journey apart from his friend; even on his deathbed, Gullikson was with Sampras. It was a courageous commitment, but with a potential payoff that couldn't be ignored, the chance that a piece of what was lost could be reclaimed, if only for a fortnight.

In simpler terms, it just seemed like the thing to do.

You know. Competing.

"Tim was such a verbal guy; de facto, he really put Pete in touch with what tennis is all about," said Peter Bodo, author and *Tennis* magazine senior writer.

"I think he gave Pete a tremendous boost and not only in terms of tennis technique and strategy. Tim made tennis real, in Pete's life.

"We all deal with things like this in our life. Life goes on. And life will go on for Pete Sampras, too. Of course, Tim will be an issue for some time and Pete will have to deal with that."

But could he? Admirable as his apparent resolve seemed when he left for Europe, he looked like anything but a French Open threat at the World Team Cup competition in Dusseldorf. He lost to Bohdan Ulihrach of the Czech Republic. Then, having hurt his back, he pulled out of a match against Richard Krajicek of The Netherlands. Finally, he was beaten in straight sets by Kafelnikov.

An undesirable start but not totally surprising since Sampras had no match time on clay beforehand and little court time. After the funeral, Annacone had accompanied him home, but Sampras couldn't bring himself to practise. The pain still was too great.

"Pete went over and played Paris on emotion," Tom Gullikson said.

That was in lieu of preparation. Thus, the question was how far emotion alone could carry him on his worst surface, at the only major tournament he hadn't won, against a field figuring — and rightfully so — that he was more vulnerable than ever.

On the other hand, the possibility existed that Sampras could somehow benefit from his mediocre French Open history — his best showings were three consecutive quarter-finals — and concoct a respectable effort.

"Pete's going to be loose in a sense," predicted John McEnroe. "He's not going to have the tremendous pressure like he felt the last couple of years. I can't speak for him, but I don't think he'll be obsessed."

Long before Gullikson's condition worsened, Sampras had decided on a less-rigorous regimen for the 1996 French. In 1995 he played extensively on clay prior to the major and somewhere along the way, decided he was a backcourter.

So after the 1996 Lipton — the fifth major, in many people's opinions — Sampras headed for Asia and the opportunity to remain on hard courts a while longer and build confidence, albeit at the price of lost clay-court time.

The Japan and Salem opens, premier hard-court tournaments held in April — Tokyo is the site of the first event, while Osaka and Hong Kong have played host to the Salem Open — have been kind to Sampras when he's made the decision to visit and postpone the red-clay grind.

On April 11, 1993, he won the Tokyo title, beating Brad Gilbert in the final. The next day he ascended to the No.1 ranking for the first time. The next weekend he won in Hong Kong, beating Courier.

In 1994, Sampras again swept the two tournaments, beating Lionel Roux in Osaka and Michael Chang — the ultimate crowd favourite, save for Japan's top player Shuzo Matsuoka — in Tokyo.

Having missed both in 1995 while trying to transform himself into Alberto Berasategui, Sampras returned in 1996 and came away with his third 'Asian double'.

As in 1993, it came with a bonus. On April 14 in Hong Kong, Sampras beat Chang in a tough three-set Salem final. The next morning he regained the No.1 ranking from Muster, who'd been there for a month. Sampras, in his 117th week as the world's top player, took the momentum to Hong Kong, where Davis Cup mate Richey Reneberg fell in a straight-set final.

Extending his personal spring hard-court swing kept Sampras in an attacking frame of mind — a positive frame of mind. Or at least as positive as could be managed with Gullikson fading.

Certainly he was in good form compared to the year before.

"I was on the clay courts so long that I lost a bit of my serve-and-volley game," Sampras said during the World Team Cup. "This time I want to play on my terms and still be aggressive on the big points."

No sign of that against Ulihrach, on a cold, damp day that suited Sampras' mind set but not his playing style.

"Mentally I feel as good as I can feel right now," Sampras said after the 7-6, 2-6, 6-3 loss, his first match since winning the final in Tokyo on April 21.

"I need to get into the swing of things. For my first match [in four weeks] it felt pretty good. It was a very weird match with many ups and downs. I was trying to hit big shots too quickly. I didn't have the patience. But it was a very important match for me since I hadn't played on clay since last year's French Open.

"I hope that with each match I can get better. I need some matches. I would certainly like to be winning [going into the French]. It gives you some confidence. That's important to get going again."

A back injury initially threatened Sampras' French participation. Treatment for what Sampras called 'blocked muscles' made him well enough to play Kafelnikov and head to Paris 0-2 on red clay but at least with two more sets in the book.

"I'm not sure what physical shape Sampras is in," McEnroe said. "But in my mind, after what he's been through with Tim, I don't think he feels a lot of pressure. Some of it comes down to luck. It might come down to the draw he gets."

Luck Of The Draw 14

SOMEONE, surely, had to be joking. This was enough to evoke McEnroe, Wimbledon 1981: "You cannot be serious!"

There are tough draws and then again, there are tough draws. But Sampras' 1996 French Open road looked too tough to believe. A first-round match against a decent Swede, Magnus Gustafsson, was tough enough. Get by that and Sampras most assuredly would face Sergi Bruguera, the French titlist in 1993-94, in the second round. Bruguera was unseeded because his world rankings had dropped outside the top 16 as he battled back from a severe ankle injury; the French Open seeding committee, going strictly by the latest ATP Tour world rankings, had excluded him from its list of placements.

A slap against Bruguera, but a potential knockout blow to Sampras. After Bruguera — talk about looking ahead — were probable matches against fellow Americans Todd Martin and Jim Courier. Win all of the above and he would be in the semi-finals still two victories away from the title.

It didn't look good. Sampras' Davis Cup final performance the preceding winter had to be viewed as a one-off, a shot in the dark, so to speak, a drama played out over a weekend and unlikely to be replayed over a two-week span.

Precedent. That's what you look for when scoping out potential champions of Grand Slam events. None could be found, linking Sampras and the French.

"I've played well there, but it's an ongoing situation I'm trying to figure out," Sampras said. "It's just difficult, difficult for me to win there. Hopefully this will be the year."

Fluke or not, Sampras was rewinding the Davis Cup final as the French approached.

"The problem I have on clay is my patience," he admitted. "It's a whole new frame of mind when I walk on clay. The way I played against Kafelnikov in the Davis Cup is the way I should play [on clay]; come in, use my strengths. I hope that match carries over six months, but we'll see. You know, I've talked so much about the French and trying to play well on clay. You just have to stop talking about it and just play."

Just play — that was Sampras' line after the draw came out. No bitching, no moaning about bad luck, a bad back or a slight cold that had cropped up just in time to make things more interesting.

Instead, Sampras presented the forthright attitude that Tim Gullikson had tapped into, then refined.

After beating Gustafsson in his first-round match, Sampras looked ahead to Bruguera, to the entire imposing bracket that amounted to an obstacle course. While accepting his fate, he did take time to point out that it was the toughest draw of his career in a Grand Slam tournament.

"Sure, I'd love to have an easier road in the first week," Sampras said. "It's the luck of the draw. Sergi is a tough match up."

Motivation aplenty, Sampras even found the nerve to talk about winning the tournament. A surprising topic to address considering the coming rounds.

"You certainly couldn't do anything more in a career than win all four of the majors, unless you do it all in one year, which is something that's very tough to do," Sampras said.

"The way I look at it, it's a big challenge, but I feel like I have the game to play well [at the French]. If it's this year, great. If it's next year, great. To one day break through and have things just kind of fall into place with who I play and how I'm playing... The French Open is one tournament that is special, because I haven't won it, obviously.

"I've always given myself a shot at the French even though I might not say it [publicly]. Deep down I feel like I can win no matter what the circumstances are."

Tim talking?

"I don't feel like an underdog. I feel like I'm the one expected to win, but not the favourite to win the tournament, but really, someone who could be very dangerous."

Sampras had been dangerous before at Roland Garros. Victories over Marc Rosset, Mal Washington, Marcelo Rios — Muster, even, in 1991's first round — showed some sort of red-clay potential.

Gullikson had preached the clay gospel, goading Sampras to pride himself on grinding through matches point by point, shot by shot, thought by thought. There had been glimmers, indicators that the gospel had sunk in. Overall, though, a project incomplete.

"On clay," Sampras said, "you have to be a bit wiser. Maybe that's something I've lacked over the past years."

Clay Pigeon, With Potential 15

O F COURSE, it would take Pete Sampras time to adjust to clay. Growing up in Palos Verdes, California, was all about hard courts. Sampras estimates that as a kid he probably played, maybe, one clay-court tournament per year. At best.

And one must consider the great conversion, conceived by Sampras' original coach, Pete Fischer. He told his charge to ditch the two-handed backhand for a one-hander that would elicit long-term results on fast surfaces like those at Wimbledon and the US Open. Looking back, was a French Open title forsaken?

Probably not. Sampras with a two-handed, grind-it-out mentality would have, in the long run, been like a painter forced to seek work in commercial art.

Sampras' clay-court results on the pro tour can be likened to his junior tournament record. Neither impressive, but both evolving.

Or was it dissolving? Improvement looked a long way off in 1989, Sampras' first French Open. After winning a first-round match he came up against Michael Chang, who was en route to winning the tournament at the age of 17 years, three months — the youngest French Open champion in history. Chang allowed Sampras only three games, one per set.

Sampras skipped the French in 1990, returning the next year for another puzzling showing. He defeated Thomas Muster in a five-set, first-round match only to then fall in straights to Frenchman Thierry Champion.

By the time the 1992 tournament came around, Sampras had begun working with Gullikson. And slowly, Sampras had begun to come around. In Paris that year, suddenly he was a contender, reaching the quarter-finals before losing to Agassi. He finished the year 23-7 on clay, playing eight tournaments.

"I understand [now] that it takes 20 to 30 balls on clay to win a point and I don't mind staying back and trading groundies," Sampras said in 1992. "Playing on clay takes a much more intense mentality, and you have to be more willing to grind it out."

In 1993, only four weeks after attaining the No.1 ranking for the first time, he suffered a four-set loss to eventual champion Sergi Bruguera.

Three consecutive major championships followed, and Sampras arrived at the 1994 French as one of the favourites, even though he had only one clay-court championship — Kitzbuhel, Austria, in 1992; beating Alberto Mancini in the final — to his credit. But that year, coming in, he had already won seven tournaments to tighten his grip on No.1.

Top-seeded at the French because of his ranking for the second consecutive year, Sampras looked ready to justify his placement. At least the potential was there to do so, and it was about time.

If only Sampras could have believed in himself a bit more. He didn't seem to. His cautiously optimistic stance had a defeatist tone that spring, before he left for Europe.

"When I walk out on clay, I feel a bit more vulnerable," Sampras said. "I think guys come out to play me on clay feeling they have a pretty good chance. Basically, my game doesn't suit the surface. My serve isn't quite as effective and when I play the guys who return well like Agassi, that's what gives me a lot of trouble.

"In order for me to play well on clay, I'm going to have to be extremely patient and choose my opportunities to come to net. But I feel like I'm getting better and better; 1992 was kind of the hump for me to get over to convince myself I could play on clay. I still have a ways to go to hopefully one day win the French. I think it's a realistic possibility, whether it's this year, next year or five years from now; I feel like one year I can come through."

Sampras defended these words, which came in a press conference, as not self-defeating but rather, "reality. I wish I didn't feel that it was but that's the way I feel. When I walk on a hard court I feel like if I play my [best] tennis I should win, whereas on clay I feel vulnerable. That's the way it is."

Assessing Sampras' chances was the most intriguing aspect of the 1994 French and almost universally, others were more positive about his chances than he was. His idol, Rod Laver — who altered his attacking game well enough to win the French twice, in 1962 and 1969 — outlined his assessment in a *Tennis* magazine article entitled, 'How Sampras Can Win the French.'

Laver's synopsis: Sampras needed to take a bit off his serve, go after his returns a little more, and get to net more than ever. Laver also preached mental toughness, pointing out that Sampras' occasional lapses had no place in the clay-court mentality.

Laver also noted Sampras' improved steadiness. At least, on that point, Sampras sounded confident.

"I feel that I can rally with anyone in the world and survive," he said. "And I feel like the French Open courts are quick enough where somebody [who attacks a lot] can win.

Sampras had just won the 1994 Australian Open, his third consecutive major championship, following his 1993 Wimbledon and US Open successes. That dominance ran its logical course leading up to the 1994 French; the talk wasn't so much about another Grand Slam title as it was about capturing *the* Grand Slam.

Grand Slam. Once upon a time, those two words described a

sweep of the year's four majors — Australian, French, Wimbledon and US — just as it did in golf (Masters, US Open, British Open and PGA). In the 1980s, the term evolved into a designation for any one of the four majors.

Perfect timing for Sampras to evoke such ramblings; 25 years earlier, Laver had won the second of his Grand Slams, seven years after his first — In between those two milestones Laver played professionally and was thus banned from the tournaments until the game went 'open' to pros and 31 years after *the* first, by Don Budge.

Aside from Budge and Laver, only three others had swept the big ones in a calendar year: Maureen 'Little Mo' Connolly in 1953, Margaret Smith Court in 1970 and Steffi Graf in 1988.

In May of 1994, Sampras sure did seem to have a chance to do it, too. What a wonderful potential story, given his feelings for Laver, and Laver's respect for Sampras' attempts to evoke the style and standards of the game's former greats.

Laver saw the hype coming, and included a crash course on dealing with it his *Tennis* magazine piece.

'The pressure one puts on oneself [in tennis] is hard to explain,' Laver wrote. 'So the less said in interviews about Pete going for the Grand Slam, the better, and... [avoiding such discussion] is what he's doing. It's better for him not to put pressure on himself.'

Especially with the media beginning to feed.

As 1994 began, many in the press already were working on 'Laver in 1969' anniversary pieces, or had them in the planning stages. A great tale under normal circumstances. Even though the men's game wasn't nearly as deep as today, it was still tough, especially from the fourth round on, at major tournaments. And what made Laver's 1969 so compelling was that he picked up where he left off in 1962.

But now, suddenly, a new angle had surfaced, then stayed afloat when Sampras won the 1994 Australian Open. There was no ducking the issue, as the French approached.

"That would definitely be something [to win the Grand Slam],"

Sampras said. "I feel like today it's a pretty tough feat to accomplish. I'm not saying I can't do it, but to win all four in one year would be more difficult to do today than when Laver did it. I'm not saying that what he did wasn't great; I mean, it would definitely be some kind of great story [to do it these days].

"[Right now] I'm just kind of taking it one match at a time at the French. That's what I'm aiming for. I'm not looking that far in the year, but [a Grand Slam] would definitely be sweet as much as I've looked up to Laver. To do what he did… well, you couldn't do more in the game."

Anything Laver did was all right with Sampras, who loves to point out that the Rocket probably would have been, like himself, considered boring by the 1990s standards that still suffer from post-McEnroe/Connors depression and have been raised artificially by Agassi's wave of commercialism.

Winning *the* Grand Slam would provide the ultimate link with Laver and, in truth, provide an ultimate defence for his alleged lack of charisma.

"I kind of think the media, probably over the last 25 to 30 years, is more concerned with your personality and what you are doing off the court than what you're doing on the court," Sampras said.

"I am sure that when Rod and Rosewall were in their heydays they played tennis and were class guys [while doing so]. That's what I am all about. Some people want me to be someone that I'm really not and I'm not going to let that happen. I'm the same person [on court as off]. I'm going to go out there and give it everything I have and try to win. If that's not good enough for some people, then that's something I'm going to have to live with."

"Putting out fire with gasoline."

Aside from being a line from an eerie David Bowie song ('Cat People — Putting Out Fire'), those five words — summed up the Grand Slam hype after Sampras travelled to Europe and won the Italian Open. In winning only his second career clay-court event, he prevented Boris Becker from winning his first.

Very big, this. Rome ain't Kitzbuhel. Rome is one notch below the majors, with a roll of past winners that includes a mix of clay-courters extraordinaire and others who were champions on any surface. Bill Tilden won the first Italian Open in 1930. Laver, Bjorn Borg and Ilie Nastase each took the title twice. And, as both inspiration and precedent for Sampras, there were the odd serve-and-volleyers to come through: Tony Roche in 1966, John Newcombe in 1969.

At the French Open, though, Sampras would go up against a history seldom kind to power players. In some ways, the French is more interesting in terms of the men who *haven't* won it, than those who have.

Look at the champion's list. Let's call it a game: Spot the volleyer. Slim pickings.

Absentees include McEnroe, who came close once, in 1984, before folding against Ivan Lendl in the final and losing in five. Newcombe? No way. Stefan Edberg lost the 1989 final to Michael Chang and never made up for it.

One must go back to 1983 to find an attacking player on the list. And even that gets an asterisk: Frenchman Yannick Noah actually was an all-court talent and could afford to take chances that year, so unnerved were his rivals by nationalistic sentiment and the unmistakable stamp of destiny that fortnight had.

Now Sampras had a shot at dealing in destiny. The Italian Open had proven his clay capability and justified the long hours he had logged back home, under the searing Florida sun, goaded by Gullikson and physical fitness guru Etcheberry.

Clay pigeon no more, Sampras flew into Paris with his confidence finally soaring, hell-bent on doing his best imitation of Laver.

Sampras hoped for an easy draw.

He didn't get it.

His first-round opponent, Alberto Costa, a 19-year-old Barcelona baseliner, was a second-year pro rising fast in the rankings. Having ended 1993 at No.221, he would shoot to No.52 by year's end and be named the ATP Tour's 1994 Newcomer of the Year.

He also knew his way around Roland Garros. The year before, in his last junior season, he reached the French Junior Boys final. At the end of 1993 he won the Orange Bowl International and finished the year No.4 in the world.

Very scary.

But Sampras, in a match that could have gotten tight if he had, won easily in straight sets, then pondered a similar task awaiting in the second round. Marcelo Rios, an 18-year-old Chilean, was a shade scarier. He was the world's No.1-ranked boy in 1993, and he had won the US Open juniors. Like Costa, his ATP ranking was on the move. Like Costa, he too went down in straight sets but not before pushing Sampras to tie-breaks in the first two, and winning over the crowd with his shot-making ability and nerve.

Such encouraging results had Sampras raring for a third-round match against Dutchman Paul Haarhuis, who in his eight years on tour had crafted a niche for knocking off ranked opponents in singles, when he wasn't busy becoming one of the world's top doubles players.

In the 1989 US Open, only his second major tournament, Haarhuis upset John McEnroe. Two years later at the Open he beat Boris Becker. In 1992 he bagged Ivan Lendl and Michael Chang. In 1993, he got Goran Ivanisevic.

He had never played Sampras before. His first look was memorable. Sampras dropped six games in a 99-minute rout, playing comfortably for the first time in the tournament. Sampras' ten aces were a moderate number. But Laver was smiling somewhere, because of the many service winners Sampras scored by taking something off.

"It makes it much easier for me when I am serving [like that]," Sampras said. "I get a lot of quick, easy points. When I'm serving well the rest of my game just carries through a bit better.

"[In this match] I played the way I can on clay. I have more confidence now. When I first got here I didn't give myself a chance [to win the tournament]. Now I feel better about it.

"I feel like I didn't hit the ball all that great the first two rounds but [his time] I hit the ball as well as I could. I didn't want to give Haarhuis an opportunity to get into his game, and I did a good job at that."

Sampras' public U-turn regarding his prospects set him up for a fall. So did the on-paper outlook of his fourth-round match. The opponent, Mikael Tillstrom, had to survive the qualifying tournament to make the main draw and was ranked 226th in the world. He had never played anyone in the top ten. And Sampras had to be thinking ahead to the probable quarter-final against Jim Courier, the French champion in 1991-92.

The first two sets went down smoothly, both 6-4 to Sampras. Incredibly, the match started to slip away at that point; Tillstrom's 6-1 third-set cruise was the first set Sampras had lost in the tournament. In the fourth set, serving at 3-4, Sampras survived four break points. He then broke at love for a 5-4 lead, served out the match, then searched for explanations.

"It wasn't pretty but I got the job done," he said. "That's the bottom line; I'm not going home yet."

Courier had his own fourth-round struggle, but came through in four sets against Oliver Delaitre, setting up 'a war', according to Sampras.

It would be the 13th Sampras-Courier meeting, with Sampras leading 10-2. But they had never played on clay, a tip on how much Sampras had struggled on the surface; he seldom lasted long enough in clay tournaments to run into Courier.

"Jim is maybe the best clay-court player in the world," Sampras acknowledged in 1993. "I'm going to have to play at a much higher level than I have been. We bring out the best in each other; if there's a tough match, this is it and you have to consider him a slight favourite. It's going to be a big challenge for me."

Too big. Courier's four-set victory illustrated the effects of red clay. Sampras' power wasn't as important. Courier got to do what he does best — stay at the baseline and slug away. Sampras got caught up in trading groundstrokes, finishing with only four winning volleys.

Gone was the hope of a Grand Slam, and of a 'non-calendar year' Grand Slam — a label for winning four consecutive majors over portions of two years. A watered-down version of the real thing, but impressive nonetheless.

"The clay limited my serve and helped out his forehand," Sampras said. "I should have attacked and come in more. I felt I had my chances."

Sampras would have been hard-pressed to win the tournament anyway. Defending champion Sergi Bruguera, not Courier, was establishing himself as the best clay-courter around. Bruguera beat Courier in the semi-finals and Alberto Berasategui in the final. Bruguera almost certainly would have handled Sampras, given his passing-shot expertise.

As the tournament closed, Sampras may have been the world's No.1 player but he wasn't in the same ballpark as Courier or Bruguera when the park had dirt underfoot.

No, he was at least a year or two — or three — away from a serious French Open run.

Maybe longer.

Sampras got it all mixed up, as he laid his 1995 French Open groundwork.

Perhaps buoyed by his solid 1994 effort that took him to the quarter-finals for the third consecutive year, he decided to jump head-first into the European clay-court season that precedes the French. Preceding that, he also committed to a Davis Cup competition on clay, in Palermo, Italy. He won both matches in a US shutout, raising his hopes for a competitive Paris fortnight.

From there he embarked on an ambitious schedule, and bombed. Playing four tournaments before the French, he lost in the first round three times, one loss via retirement due to a twisted ankle. A semi-final at Hamburg was the highlight of this ill-fated swing. If that sentence doesn't say it all...

A tough first-round match awaited Sampras in Paris: Gilbert Schaller, an Austrian clay specialist who, at No.24 in the world, was on the outskirts of seeding consideration. Schaller doesn't have much going for him other than a lifetime supply of consistency. But that bodes well on clay, against an opponent not at home to begin with and lacking confidence to boot.

Schaller's shocker — a five-set victory from 2-1 down, played out over two days — sent Sampras packing, again, for Tampa. Sent him home to regroup for Wimbledon and the grass courts that suddenly looked very inviting.

"I think this loss is probably going to sit with me for quite a while," Sampras said. "I changed my whole schedule to play more on clay this time and to improve my clay-court game. To come up against a tough opponent in the first round… I had some chances but just came up a little bit short. That's the way my whole clay-court season kind of went. This was just icing on the cake."

Sampras maintained that he still had a grip on clay-court tennis despite the disastrous spring. He blamed his serve, the ignition switch to his game no matter the surface. "The worse I serve the more I struggle on clay," he said.

This wasn't devastation, but it wasn't far off. Sampras was irked enough to repel an innocuous post-match press-conference inquiry. Since April 1995, Sampras had flown back to Tampa from Europe four times. He would make his fifth trip the next day, for a break before Wimbledon. The reporter wanted to know if all the travel and jet lag may have hurt his efforts, and he was specifically wondering why Sampras would go home with Wimbledon only three weeks away. "Aren't you asking too much of your body?" he asked.

Sampras' response: "That is one of the worst questions I have heard."

After a quick reiteration, Sampras went on, saying, "What am I going to do, hang out here? [I guess] I'll just hang out in the locker room. I mean, I'm not going to hang out in Europe."

Too Much To Ask 16

LESS is more. That summarised Sampras' new-and-hopefully-improved approach for the 1996 French Open. There would be no repeat of 1995 when he got the wild-eyed notion that he was Bjorn Borg reincarnated and proceeded to enter every European event in sight leading up to the French. Sampras had decided to go in the other direction and see as little red clay as possible.

Weird stuff, but what the hell, he figured. The other way sure didn't work. And besides, with Gullikson's condition worsening daily, a lower-key clay campaign made sense for other reasons.

Sampras thus determined that the Italian Open and the World Team Cup, held on the two weeks immediately preceding Paris, would be enough; Gullikson's death eliminated the Italian.

The reasoning behind this reflects Sampras' image among his fellow players as an artistic sort. Sampras, perhaps more than any other player on the tour these days, doesn't play tennis as much as he *feels* tennis. His talent is instinctive. And it was instinct that jolted Sampras into seeing the error of his 1995 ways.

Now he had it straight:

More had been less.

Sampras wasn't Sampras in the spring of 1995. Overloading on clay had backfired. He lapsed into the generic clay-court style that is incongruous with his strengths. He started attacking less, rallying more. No wonder he struggled.

Thus, the pronouncement that in 1996 he would play the French 'on my terms'. Win or lose, there would be no reasonable facsimile of Pete Sampras. Observers could expect the staples: big serves and probing returns — particularly with the backhand chip-and-charge designed to break up rallies or negate a meaty serve — plus lots of net coverage.

The first-round victory over Magnus Gustafsson set the tone. Sampras had 23 aces — three in the first game of the match — and lost his serve only once. On a cloudy, mid-50's, rain-delayed day not conducive to power, this was impressive, indeed.

"Those were tough conditions," Sampras said. "Very heavy and slow. It was tough to serve and volley."

Gustafsson didn't notice Sampras having problems.

"I don't think I'll get that many aces the whole year," he cracked.

Meanwhile, Sampras' attacking off the return heavily sliced backhands down the line, in the deuce court, were special gems — led him to four breaks of the Swede.

Via his terms.

"I'm trying to [play that way]," Sampras said. "Trying to be aggressive, not be so passive like I have been in the past. I need to play my normal game, but in control. It's a fine line I'm trying to figure out."

Sampras' synopsis of the fine line:

"I come to a point in a match on clay when it's kind of tough, to put guys away. Do I serve and volley? Do I stay back? You want to be aggressive but you don't want to come in on the wrong ball. You have to be much more selective on the shots to be aggressive on. When I get in trouble on clay I start pressing. I'm six feet behind the baseline going for winners. Things on hardcourt or indoors I take for granted. This year I'm trying to play a little smarter."

Bruguera — now there's an intelligence test on clay. The

champion in 1993-94, Bruguera lost in the 1995 semi-finals to Michael Chang and had since been hampered by injuries. He came into the French with a 9-9 1996 record, but he still was considered a threat, if not a force.

Most certainly was he a threat to Sampras. Bruguera held a 2-1 head-to-head edge, both victories on clay, including the 1993 French semis. Few people gave Sampras much of a chance. And he didn't sound very upbeat about it, either.

Something else to consider: Sampras' mind set. During the Gustafsson match, his body language suggested depression. Sampras stalked slowly around the court between points, his shoulder stoop more evident than usual. His look was solemn, solitary.

Tim Gullikson had been dead only 24 days.

"It's been difficult," Sampras said. "I'd rather not comment too much on it. I'll probably start tearing up. It's tough to talk about. It's so soon."

The emotion that Tom Gullikson said Sampras was running on had been more than adequate for Gustafsson. But there was so much more tennis to be played.

The line on Bruguera: great groundies, surprising serve, best pack a lunch. You're signing up for the duration, playing this guy.

He presented so many tests for Sampras. The fact that they were matched in the second round was another example of why the various major tournaments should seed based on the peculiarities of their event rather than the world rankings. Wimbledon does its own thing, avoiding the embarrassment of a grass-court dud being favoured over someone with past success on the surface. It was criminal for Bruguera to be excluded from the 16 seeds because his world ranking had fallen to No.23.

Sampras opened the match with an ace, but in contrast to the first round he would harness his big guns for the most part, using placement to keep his cagey foe off balance.

In exactly one hour, Sampras swept through the first two sets, 6-3, 6-4, playing serve-and-volley all the way, "probably the best serve-and-volley tennis I've ever played," Sampras said.

Then, the lack of match time caught up with him slightly. He tired, got spooked in a tie-break and lost 7-2. Bruguera, recharged, showed his past championship form in running through the fourth set 6-2.

The fifth hinged on a second-game service break of Bruguera. Sampras got five break points before cashing in. The game lasted 14 points; it ended with Sampras charging, then caressing a backhand drop volley for a winner. Sampras, up 2-0, ran out the set 6-3.

"This is my best [French Open] win by far," Sampras said. "To beat someone of Sergi's capabilities on clay, someone who's won here twice before gives me some confidence that I can play with the Brugueras and whoever is across the net [on clay]. The match had a lot of emotion, a lot of everything."

It had 20 break-point opportunities that came Bruguera's way; he converted only two. There's your key statistic. Try two others: Sampras had 43 service winners and got 59 per cent of his first serves in.

"My serve was the key," Sampras said. "If you can serve that well and consistently, and volley crisply, you can play well on clay. My serve was the foundation. It made my returning games a little looser because I was holding pretty easily."

Sampras sacrificed some service power — he had a relatively low 14-ace total, same as his opponent — for percentages. Bruguera said he'd never seen Sampras serve better. Nor, he added, had he seen anyone serve like that lately.

Bruguera stopped short of giving Sampras full due, making sure to mention a foot injury that he said was slowing him just enough to be troublesome. Bruguera's input wasn't needed, though, to judge this as one of Sampras' career highlights.

"As far as a second-round match, this was the toughest one I've ever had to get through at a Grand Slam tournament," Sampras said. "I'm still hanging around, but there are so many other potential winners here. Same old cliché: It's one match at a time. I don't look ahead."

Hard to believe, considering that in Sampras' half, entering the third round were three ominous, probable opponents: Todd Martin, Courier and Yevgeny Kafelnikov.

Martin and Sampras are good friends and big hitters who invariably hook up in arduous struggles virtually devoid of rallies, much less drama. Their third-round match at the French fit neatly into that mould, with Sampras winning in five sets, in the face of 29 Martin aces.

Next up: a break, more or less, in the form of young Australian Scott Draper. After three strong sets, Sampras looked ahead to another match with Courier, whom he had beaten the last four times they'd played.

"Trying to control the points [will be tough]," Sampras said. "Jim serves big enough that he controls the centre of the court and hits the big forehand. I need to keep the ball away from the centre of the court, be offensive, mix it up. Kind of like I did against Bruguera. Show him a different look, trying to be as aggressive as I can on clay."

Talk of going all the way had started to creep into Sampras' post-match interviews, as had roundabout questions regarding Tim Gullikson. A fortnight image: man on a mission. One reporter even came up with the notion that Sampras was destined to win, that he might be getting some other-worldly help, as in Gullikson's spirit. He had the nerve to ask Courier if he thought that possible.

"Maybe... or... maybe not," Courier said.

The help that Sampras was getting, that actually could be seen, was coming from Paul Annacone, now coaching Sampras solo since Gullikson's death. "Paul's done a real good job in a tough situation," Tom Gullikson said. Former ATP Tour trainer Todd Snyder, now Sampras' personal fitness man, also was along.

Sampras came into the French wanting to come to net more than ever. No one could be better to advise on that than Annacone, a serve-and-volleyer who reached the world's top 20 in the 1980s.

"He came in on everything — *everything*," Sampras jokes.

It was a team approach that left little time for anything but tennis, even though Mulcahy was along. Sampras looked incredulous when asked how he was spending time away from the tournament, because he was spending it much like he does at every tournament, in his hotel room or looking for decent restaurants, like the pizza place he and Todd Martin found during the tournament's first week, on the Champs-Elysees.

"We ate a lot," Martin said, deadpan.

Sampras stayed at an upscale hotel, situated less than 30 minutes drive from Roland Garros. It was a better arrangement than in 1995, when he stayed at the Meredien. Sampras was given a room near the elevator, and the noise was considerable. He objected and got another room but as it turned out, didn't need it long. Maybe Gilbert Schaller (whom Sampras lost to in the first round of the 1995 French Open) had connections at the Meredien.

A Meredien manager said the room ruckus had nothing to do with the hotel switch. "He lost last year and he didn't want to come back to the same place because of that," she said.

A new Nike-Agassi commercial has this hook: "If you're not at a tournament to win, then you're a tourist." It's a marketing slogan that could apply just as easily to Sampras. He's no tourist, and that's why he treats suggestions that he acts like one almost with disdain.

"Unfortunately, tennis is the main priority," Sampras said. "If I'm not [at Roland Garros], I'm either resting or practising. There's not a lot of time to go out and sight-see. Tennis is why I'm here. It's not a vacation. This is my job. I just do what I have to do to prepare."

His preparation during the tournament was solid. His practice partner was Thierry Guardiola, a 23-year-old Frenchman whose highest world ranking is No.111, but who knows his way around the clay. Guardiola hits a good ball, without excessive top-spin — perfect for a big hitter's workout.

On off days, Sampras typically showed up at Roland Garros around 1pm, with a court reserved for at least 90 minutes. He, Annacone and Snyder would calmly show up, oblivious to the trail of fans following after them. Guardiola and his coach likewise were given cursory glances. Nary a word would be spoken, and the practice commenced. Simple, but structured: a good 30 minutes of baseline trading, followed by one-up/one-back exchanges, some serving and, finally, playing out some points.

On match days, Sampras showed up earlier, around 11am, with a one-hour reservation. Sometimes, the workouts would be cut short if Sampras felt sufficiently loose.

Sampras' racquets at the French — and Wimbledon —were strung between 78-80 pounds (34-35 kilos) but all at slightly different tensions. Typically at these tournaments, and at most others, he has ten racquets on hand. He needs ten. He breaks strings regularly, because of the high tension he prefers. That puts the Babolat stringers on site (Babolat makes VS gut, Sampras' string of choice) under the gun. Word is the Babolat stringers at the French Open are not great fans of Sampras; with the number of groundstrokes hit each match, with the clay working its way between the strings, rubbing them raw, Sampras' string-breaking reaches absurd proportions.

"I've stressed out enough on the court with breaking strings, worrying if I have enough racquets," Sampras said. "I decided this year that I was going to bring ten and string them all up. I string my racquets very tight with very thin gut. [Breaking strings] is the price I pay for the way I string them. That's the only way I like my racquets."

Sampras is so finicky about his strings that, like Ivan Lendl before him, he insists on having his racquets strung the morning of a match.

During each practice, Annacone patrolled the back of Sampras' court, holding a racquet as all coaches do, even though they may use it but once during the session. Whatever he and Sampras said to each other, only they heard. But there never seemed to be much give-and-take. 'An agenda of restraint' is what *Tennis* magazine's Pete Bodo calls Annacone's coaching situation. Sampras is a player requiring a long leash.

Likewise, Snyder knows he's doing a good job when his workload drops. Snyder, though, was busy in Paris.

Sampras was in need of more than one massage during the event.

This edition of Sampras-Courier featured 53 games. One stood out as crucial. Fourth set, Courier led 4-3, up 2-1 in sets; Sampras served and went down 15-40. He saved one break point with an ace. At 30-40, the first serve flew wildly as he snapped a string.

Slowly, deliberately, Sampras walked to the side, picked up a new racquet and returned to the service line, whereupon he cracked a second-serve ace in the corner of the ad court, on the line no less.

Sampras held, then broke Courier and went on to even the match at two sets apiece. The fifth set was decided by a third-game break of Courier. Sampras ended the proceedings with his 28th ace — Courier had 29 — to wrap up a 6-7 (4-7), 4-6, 6-4, 6-4, 6-4 victory.

"I thought about our match in the Australian Open," Sampras said, referring to the 1995 Aussie quarter-finals when Courier also won the first two sets only to see Sampras come back.

"I did it once before and [I thought] there's no reason, even though this is on clay, that I can't do it again. I felt I was hitting the ball well. I was serving well. I was just kind of over-anxious. It was one of those matches where I wasn't going to give it to him."

For the first time during the tournament, Sampras showed signs of serious fatigue. It was his third five-set match, and his expression relayed that. Sampras looked ready to pass out for most of the last set, yet he kept firing.

Courier wasn't surprised.

"I've seen it before," Courier began. "Pete's a good actor, let's put it that way. Some people put up a front that they're tough. Pete tends to put up a front that he's hurting but he still seems to fire those aces. He's tough. I don't pay much attention to him when he's looking tired, because I know it really doesn't matter, with his serve, it really doesn't make much difference what he looks like."

"I was tired, yeah," Sampras countered, confronted with Courier's allegations. "In the middle of the fourth and fifth set, at that point it was just adrenalin. My legs were feeling heavy. I didn't have quite the spring that I had in the first couple of sets. The long matches I've played maybe took its toll. Fortunately, the court was playing reasonably quick and my serve just kind of won it for me.

So closed another chapter in the increasingly one-sided Sampras-Courier rivalry. This latest victory gave Sampras a 15-3 edge, almost inconceivable considering how many of the matches have been close, plus the fact that Courier is a former No.1-ranked player.

"I just have to get over the hump," Courier said. "My record [against him] is never going to get better unless I keep playing him. I've got to keep playing him, take my chances and hopefully it will come around for me.

"I'm a big believer in what goes around, comes around. Well, what's gone around sure as hell better come back around soon."

Sampras' next opponent, Yevgeny Kafelnikov, had payback on his mind after the previous December's Davis Cup final and the punishments he absorbed in singles and doubles. Kafelnikov defeated Sampras in the World Team Cup prior to the French, but that was insignificant, Sampras said.

"It's going to be a completely different match. I know what to expect and vice versa. I know what he likes. I've beaten him before so there's no reason why I can't do it again."

Kafelnikov proceeded to the final unhindered by either his opponents or the glare of media attention, even though, in his own right, he was a major story, a player fulfilling the potential everyone knew he possessed.

Kafelnikov, then 21, is nicknamed 'Kalashnikov', after a Russian rifle. Kafelnikov's forehand is the basis for that association, but his game is truly all-court. Coming into the French he was ranked sixth in the world, seeded fifth with fifth-ranked Boris Becker out due to injury.

In reaching the final he lost one set, and that one a tie-breaker, to Richard Krajicek in the quarter-finals. A foreboding contrast, it was, to Sampras' two weeks of hellish toil. But with two days in between quarters and semis, Sampras, one would think, would recover adequately for another round of red-dirt warfare, motivated by the prospect of making the final and the memory of the Davis Cup hammering he inflicted on the young Russian.

But there also was the chance of a let-down. Honestly. Beating Courier, while becoming a habit, takes a lot out of Sampras each and every time. They've played so many times, are virtually the same age — Courier is five days shy of being exactly a year older — and both turned pro in 1988. And, of course, they've both reached the No.1 ranking. Each match is an attempt by both at some sort of statement, if only to each other. Good friends, they nonetheless have a burning desire to beat each other. Their battles are personal, but in a sporting kind of way.

If Sampras revived his desire, there would be the question of his endurance, which had to be depleted after three five-setters. After Courier, Sampras described his 'gas tank' as "not on empty. The two days [before the semis] will be good for me to get some energy back. The extra day off certainly helps. [My engine] is still running. There's still a little bit of gas left."

And what of his mental, spiritual state? The Gullikson thing was getting heavier. After the Courier match, Sampras was asked about Gullikson during a French television interview. He broke down, sobbing, his emotions exposed publicly for the first time in the fortnight. His press conference with print media was delayed while he regained his composure. A carefully worded question was asked, avoiding direct mention of Gullikson, regarding Sampras' emotions at reaching the semis, a career-best.

"Certainly a lot of different thoughts were in my mind, good ones and some sad ones," he replied. "I fought hard, and that's really what people around me can be proud of, is that I fought."

Five matches complete, such fights had proven the ultimate testimony to Gullikson.

The tournament, though, wasn't over.

Kafelnikov's confidence, as he and Sampras warmed up on Court Central, had to be tempered by the temperature. High 80s. With no rain in sight and a mid-afternoon start, conditions favoured Sampras who, along with finalist Michael Stich and semi-finalist Marc Rosset, had been part of a servers' coming-out party at this supposedly backcourt gathering.

When Sampras started the match by holding and aceing Kafelnikov once, the party was on again. But Kafelnikov also was up for some fun. He matched Sampras hold for hold through 6-6, never facing a break point. Sampras faced two, one in the seventh game, another in the 11th. Both were survived, thanks to Kafelnikov errors.

Sampras opened the tie-breaker with an ace, and went up 2-1 with a 'mini-break' when the Russian sliced a backhand deep. But any thoughts that the set was in hand eroded on the next point when Sampras double-faulted, a terribly mistimed mistake.

Sampras made up for that, though, with another mini-break, hitting a clutch backhand volley winner for 4-3. He then stepped up to serve — a most desirable scenario.

Over the course of the next 90 seconds, the tie-breaker got away, on two uncharacteristic Sampras forehand errors. The match, the tournament, the *mission,* followed closely behind.

Sampras immediately shifted into mope mode; Kafelnikov noticed and went into high gear. The Russian raced through the last two sets 6-0, 6-2 in 45 minutes. Sampras spent most of that time with his head hung, lifting his gaze only to play half-hearted points that nearly turned the crowd against him. The French kept their trademark derisive whistling in check, but the murmuring during changeovers, a cacophony of disappointment and dismay, was just as telling.

Sampras appeared to be saying the hell with it, letting the match go. "To be honest, I was shocked," said one longtime observer and friend who asked not to be identified because he didn't want his name next to the words, "Pete quit."

"I think Pete just hit the wall, after he lost the first set," Tom

Gullikson said. "The accumulation of 14 hours on the court in his first five matches was kind of his undoing.

"When you're playing on emotion, you're going to run out eventually."

But to this extent? Sampras had only nine aces, none during his second-set walkabout. In place of aces, Sampras recorded nine double-faults. His improved returning took the afternoon off; he never reached a break point against Kafelnikov's solid, but not spectacular serve. Thirty-four unforced errors completed the self-screwing.

It was perhaps Sampras' all-time collapse. It looked even worse against the backdrop of his previous five efforts.

"The balloon popped after the first set," Sampras said. "I was very, very tired. I came into the tournament not in the best shape, and the long matches over the past week and a half [added up]. It's so disappointing because I fought so hard to get here."

His claim to fatigue didn't make complete sense, since after the third-round victory over Martin, he talked about being relatively fresh, that he could have maybe played longer, even though he'd just finished five sets.

After the Courier match, played on the tournament's second Tuesday, Sampras took a day off. On a Thursday afternoon he hit for an hour. Friday morning he knocked around for another 30 minutes.

"I felt fine," he said. "Felt pretty good in the first set. But even if I would have won the first set, I still think I was going to get tired eventually because of the heat. It still was going to be a long road to winning the match. Maybe a cooler day would have helped."

For a Florida resident to claim he was bothered by the heat, well, that happens about as often as Russians pass up vodka.

Kafelnikov, still two days away from even thinking about celebration, thought Sampras was hurt, so negative was his body language — a factor that Sampras dismissed. But the Russian, so cocky the previous December prior to and during the Davis Cup final, when he ripped Sampras' clay-court skills, went above and beyond in recognising something wasn't right with his opponent.

"Everybody knows how quick Pete is on the court," Kafelnikov said. "I think something was happening with him, for sure. Maybe his back. But he was not the Pete we're used to seeing on the court.

"Today I felt like I had a small chance to beat Pete. I just put everything together, was focused all during the match. And you know, it happened. I beat him three straight sets."

Kafelnikov was outstanding, but Sampras derived small consolation from that. The source for whatever solace he could find had to come from his five previous victories, especially over Bruguera, and the fact that he could carry on as long as he did, while dealing with the image of Tim Gullikson in a casket, a casket that he helped carry to its final resting spot.

"Pete was obviously very stressed," observed *Tennis* magazine's Pete Bodo. "You can get down on him for his performance against Kafelnikov but there really is 'a wall' for players."

And like Tom Gullikson, Bodo felt Sampras ran smack-dab into it.

Sampras was left to pick up the pieces, and at least some fairly good-sized chunks of encouragement could be found.

"In some ways, I'm obviously very disappointed to come so close to having a chance to win here," he said, "but under the circumstances I felt like I fought as hard as I could fight and beat some really good players. I can come out of here feeling good about my clay-court game. So many emotional matches... I just came out and just didn't have it like I had it the other days. [I've never been this tired] mentally, physically and emotionally, probably in my whole career. I've felt physically tired after some long matches in the summer, but I think this is probably the worst I've felt."

As proof, Sampras pulled out of the Queen's Club grass-court tournament in London starting the next week. "I've decided to go home, put the racquet up and not see a court — especially a clay court."

Sampras–Courier: Head To Head

Pete Sampras has dominated Jim Courier when it comes to victories, but his career edge obscures the fact that virtually all of their matches have been incredibly close.

Sampras–Courier

As of August 1996: Sampras 15, Courier 3

Year	Tournament	Surface	Round	Winner	Score
1988	Scottsdale	Hard	2nd	Sampras	6-3, 6-1
1991	Cincinnati	Hard	SF	Sampras	6-2, 7-5
1991	Indianapolis	Hard	SF	Sampras	6-3, 7-6
1991	US Open	Hard	QF	Courier	6-2, 7-6, 7-6
1991	ATP Finals	Carpet	F	Sampras	3-6, 7-6, 6-3, 6-4
1992	Indianapolis	Hard	F	Sampras	6-4, 6-4
1992	US Open	Hard	SF	Sampras	6-1, 3-6, 6-2, 6-2
1992	ATP Finals	Carpet	SF	Courier	7-6, 7-6
1993	Hong Kong	Hard	F	Sampras	6-3, 6-7, 7-6
1993	Wimbledon	Grass	F	Sampras	7-6, 7-6, 3-6, 6-3
1994	Australian Open	Hard	SF	Sampras	6-3, 6-4, 6-4
1994	Lipton	Hard	SF	Sampras	6-4, 7-6
1994	French Open	Clay	QF	Courier	6-4, 5-7, 6-4, 6-4
1995	Australian Open	Hard	QF	Sampras	6-7, 6-7, 6-3, 6-4, 6-3
1995	US Open	Hard	SF	Sampras	7-5, 4-6, 6-4, 7-5
1995	Essen	Carpet	QF	Sampras	6-2, 7-6
1995	Paris Open	Carpet	SF	Sampras	6-4, 3-6, 6-3
1996	French Open	Clay	QF	Sampras	6-7, 4-6, 6-4, 6-4, 6-4

Gap In The Resumé 17

CAN SAMPRAS ever win the French Open? Will he ever get as good a chance as in 1996? As Sampras noted himself after losing to Kafelnikov, "Everything has to be right for me, from my draw to the weather conditions. Hopefully one year all that happens and I can win here."

The fact that Sampras still talks about draws and conditions — factors he can't control — amounts to a peek at his psyche. Normally Sampras worries only about Sampras, figuring if he takes care of himself that nothing, or nobody, can keep him from winning. When he starts listing prerequisites, it's a very bad sign.

The weather was terrible in his first-round match against Gustafsson. Didn't matter. His draw was unbearable, yet he ripped through it, knocking off two former champions.

Bodo may be closer to the truth. He gives Sampras a good chance to win the French. But Bodo has his own prerequisite.

"The biggest stumbling block, unlike a lot of other players, is going to be the question of Pete's fitness," Bodo said, several hours before Kafelnikov finished off Michael Stich in the final, also in straight sets.

"Pete's surprisingly fragile. But I actually think he will win it He's too good a player not to. It's hard to say he will [definitely] win it but I think he *can*. Every great fast-court player has had a shot at the French. It's [not] like they can't win here. They can.

"But... this year was actually a great, great chance."

Colleague Mark Winters, a long-time Sampras follower and, despite journalism's unwritten rule of impartiality, a Sampras supporter, also mourned the loss of a prime opportunity.

Winters is less convinced that Sampras can win at Roland Garros, but adds, "I don't believe in 'nevers,' although I think there are golden times."

Which sometimes get tarnished.

"I don't think Pete's going to get a better year than this one," Winters said. "But — if it was anybody other than Pete Sampras we were talking about, I would say the guy had shot his wad, as it were.

"The Kafelnikov match, I think, shows a physical fragility on his part that must be dealt with. And the mental... well, the match seemed almost like the old days when he was first starting out on the tour."

John McEnroe cracked in all phases, in the 1984 French final against Ivan Lendl. McEnroe won the first two sets easily, lost his concentration in the third set after one of his infamous outbursts, and dropped the next three sets. He never made the final again.

While Sampras dislikes clay courts, McEnroe almost despises them. But McEnroe's criticisms apply, when considering Sampras' struggles on the surface.

"Clay takes away from the big hitters and gives players one more swing at the ball, swings they might not get on another court," McEnroe said. "In my opinion, the quality of tennis is not as high. Physical fitness comes into play more. It's a matter of just hanging in there, that's more important.

"It's impossible to answer [whether Sampras will win the French]. But a guy with his kind of ability, it's impossible to say he'll never win it."

Pete Fischer, ever the puppet-master, knows what he would do, were he still at the controls. He'd start by trying to wean Sampras from his addiction to power. Fischer doesn't completely buy into Sampras striving to play serve-and-volley at all times.

"He keeps saying he wants to do it on 'his terms' and maybe that's the right way to do it — and maybe not," Fischer said.

"After he beat Courier, I thought he was going to win it. He can win it, but there's going to have to be a change in his mind set — make that a *lot* of change in his mind set. Pete can win it but his attitude has to be a little more juvenile. He can stay out there and hit 50 balls in a row into the court. There's no reason he can't. He did it when he was a kid. Laver — who was a better serve-and-volleyer than Pete will ever be — stayed back at the French, and he did all right.

"At the French this time he had the hardest draw ever imagined. Then, after getting through the hardest draw ever imagined, he started saying things that I wouldn't have wanted him to say, like about thinking that he could win it. You never say that."

Not that Sampras ever sounded cocky during the fortnight. He certainly had a right to, though, considering his five-match sprint. In the long run, those matches will stand as some of Sampras' finest tennis, despite the semi-final when, according to Fischer, "he didn't look like he showed up."

"I've made some gains here," Sampras said. "I've come a long way on the clay over the past six or seven years. [Winning] is certainly in my sights. I'm still going to play this game for quite a while so hopefully one year it will kind of come together.

"But it was close this year. Winning the French wasn't something realistically I wanted to win when I was a kid, growing up.

"Now it is."

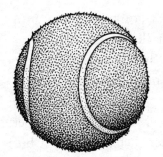

French Open Record Pete Sampras

At the age of 25, the French Open is the only Grand Slam title Pete Sampras hasn't won. He'll spend the rest of his career trying to avoid obsessing over this, while upping his intensity at the event.

French Open Record

1989
| First round | Defeated Jorge Lozano | 6-3, 6-2, 6-4 |
| Second round | Lost to Michael Chang | 6-1, 6-1, 6-1 |

1990
Did not play

1991
| First round | Defeated Thomas Muster | 4-6, 4-6, 6-4, 6-1, 6-4 |
| Second round | Lost to Thierry Champion | 6-3, 6-1, 6-1 |

1992
First round	Defeated Marc Rosset	7-6, 4-6, 6-4, 3-6, 6-3
Second round	Defeated Laurent Prades	7-6, 6-4, 7-6
Third round	Defeated Rodolphe Gilbert	6-3, 6-2, 6-3
Fourth round	Defeated Carl-Uwe Steeb	6-4, 6-3, 6-2
Quarter-finals	Lost to Andre Agassi	7-6, 6-2, 6-1

1993
First round	Defeated Andrei Cherkasov	6-1, 6-2, 3-6, 6-1
Second round	Defeated Marcos Ondruska	7-5, 6-0, 6-3
Third round	Defeated Jonas Svensson	6-4, 6-4, 6-2
Fourth round	Defeated Mal Washington	6-3, 7-6, 6-1
Quarter-finals	Lost to Sergi Bruguera	6-3, 4-6, 6-1, 6-4

1994
First round	Defeated Alberto Costa	6-3, 6-4, 6-4
Second round	Defeated Marcelo Rios	7-6, 7-6, 6-4
Third round	Defeated Paul Haarhuis	6-1, 6-4, 6-1
Fourth round	Defeated Mikael Tillstrom	6-4, 6-4, 1-6, 6-4
Quarter-finals	Lost to Jim Courier	6-4, 5-7, 6-4, 6-4

1995

| First round | Lost to Gilbert Schaller | 7-6, 4-6, 6-7, 6-2, 6-4 |

1996

First round	Defeated Magnus Gustafsson	6-1, 7-5, 7-6
Second round	Defeated Sergi Bruguera	6-3, 6-4, 6-7, 2-6, 6-3
Third round	Defeated Todd Martin	3-6, 6-4, 7-5, 4-6, 6-2
Fourth round	Defeated Scott Draper	6-4, 7-5, 6-2
Quarter-finals	Defeated Jim Courier	6-7, 4-6, 6-4, 6-4, 6-4
Semi-finals	Lost to Yevgeny Kafelnikov	7-6, 6-0, 6-2

Career won-lost: 19-7

Part V
Wimbledon

Four-Pete? 18

S AMPRAS swears that hard courts are his favourite surface. But after losing in the French Open semi-finals, grass was looking pretty good.

Wimbledon, dead ahead. Sampras, three-time defending champion and winner of 21 consecutive matches on the All-England Lawn Tennis and Croquet Club's immaculate greenery, would be back in his element, that hard court nonsense aside.

Souvenir hawkers were on alert, busy with behind-the-scenes planning of the Pete Sampras "Four-Peat" — or would it be "Four-Pete"? — T-shirt.

Discussing Wimbledon immediately brightened Sampras' spirits, after his French loss to Kafelnikov.

"I need some rest right now, mentally and physically, to get geared up to hopefully make it a 'Four-Pete'," he said. "That's what I've got to try to do, try to rebound as best I can."

Having withdrawn from the Queen's Club event, Sampras flew home with Delaina. He stayed in Tampa until the following weekend, practising on hard courts even though first-rate grass courts were at his disposal at Saddlebrook Resort, near his home. The hard courts were needed to recapture his fast-court timing. After that was accomplished, Sampras would start dealing with the precocious nature of grass-court bounces.

"I'll get back to London, walk into those gates at the All-England Club, get those feelings and those good memories," he said. "And hopefully, I'll come out ahead there."

Sampras is a creature of habit on the road. He craves familiarity in his food and lodging. During the Wimbledon fortnights, he has come find such comfort at the St James Court Hotel, where he annually rents a flat and bunkers in.

He has said that the St James is like coming home, one of the few places where he feels comfortable enough to fully unpack his suitcase. Of course, part of the reason he feels so comfortable is that he knows he'll likely be around for a while.

During the 1996 Wimbledon, Sampras bunkered in and tried to get into soccer, admittedly a stretch. But the European Championships were better than the rest of the British television line-up. Sampras doesn't care for British TV, so the soccer was at least something different.

"It's grown on me a bit," Sampras said during Wimbledon, adding that one game — England-Holland — was particularly exciting, or at least interesting. "It was like every five minutes there was a score. That was nice to see. But it is hard to sit down and watch a whole game. I think it's a different sport than what we're used to seeing in the United States."

Upon coming to England, Sampras, with Annacone's help and Snyder's supervision, went about acclimating himself to grass, a surface that he has come to appreciate, as he has come to realise how rewarding it can be to his game.

And, when cast against the arduous two weeks of toil at Roland Garros, it's an acclimation completely welcomed by Sampras. There's something soulful about grass-court tennis, as compared to clay-court tennis, and he has tapped into that.

To assist the acclimation, Sampras chose Todd Martin as his primary practice partner. A perfect choice, given the surface, and the circumstances of the previous two months. Martin, a fine grass-court player, also was a good friend of Sampras and the Gullikson family. Martin supplied the right touches of ability and kinship. Sampras needed both during this Wimbledon.

Just as the St James' attraction was familiarity, same deal for the All-England Club. Annacone said it also was like a homecoming, to the point that Sampras was ready to truly enjoy pre-tournament workouts.

"Pete's the kind of player who has to feel good about what he's doing," Annacone told *The New York Times*. "Even in practice, he's not a nose-to-the-grindstone guy like Courier. He's more artistic, so the preparation on grass suits him well because it's not about repetition."

What it comes down to is that Sampras, at Wimbledon, is secure. And the security, while based on his success, isn't truly dependent on it. Win or lose, Sampras has merged with the tournament. Were Wimbledon a lover, they would be soulmates.

That secure feeling was shaken slightly when the Wimbledon 1996 draw came out. Sampras got it stuck to him again.

His road wasn't as tough as at the French, but it still looked incredibly bumpy. His first-round opponent, Davis Cup mate Richey Reneberg, was dangerous. His probable second-round match, in terms of danger, jumped off the Richter. There, Sampras surely would encounter Mark Philippoussis, his bane at the Australian Open.

Only the beginning.

The luck of the draw had loaded up the top half of the 128-player bracket with proficient serve-and-volleyers. The bottom half belonged to baseliners, save for second-seed Boris Becker, a three-time Wimbledon titlist whose seeding was, out of respect for his grass play, four spots higher than his world ranking.

For the top-seeded Sampras to even make the final, he would have to emerge from a crowd that included 1991 champion Michael Stich, two-time runner-up Goran Ivanisevic and powerful Richard Krajicek.

No, a fourth title would not be easy. But then, what had been easy for Sampras in 1996? On the other hand, could any tennis match seem like that big of a deal, after seeing Tim Gullikson lose the ultimate battle? Sampras certainly had perspective in his corner. How this was going to shake out over the course of two weeks was hard to tell.

Finally, Sampras was coming around, able to talk about the loss.

HBO Television assembled a touching tribute to Gullikson, in which Sampras opened up.

"I thought of Tim every match I played [at the French Open]," Sampras told HBO's Frank Deford. "[His death] opened my eyes to a lot of things. It was really scary and I didn't like it. Tim was a great guy, with not a bad bone in his body and he's been taken away. I don't understand why that happened."

Given his emotional state and his lack of a Wimbledon warm-up event, Sampras maybe wasn't the smart pick, although he was the betting house favourite. Many were going with Becker, loser to Sampras in the 1995 final, based on his overpowering march to the Queen's Club title. Stich, the surprising French Open runner-up, also had plenty of support, as did his pre-tournament, part-time practice partner, Ivanisevic.

Sampras did have history on his side — and in the distance, beckoning. He was trying to become only the second man in the modern era to win four consecutive Wimbledons; Bjorn Borg got five straight in 1976-80.

T-shirt vendors awaited the outcome.

The wait for a renewal of the Sampras-Agassi rivalry would be longer. Agassi, amid a shocking slump that began earlier in the year around the time he and girlfriend Brooke Shields announced marriage plans, lost in the first round to qualifier Doug Flach, the world's 281st-ranked player, a mere 278 spots below Agassi.

Agassi played in a long-sleeved Nike shirt with a zipper front, but he was a listless billboard for his prime sponsor. At least the nightshirt effect was somewhat fitting, as Flach turned out the lights with a four-set victory.

"I just let it slip away," Agassi said. "I wasn't hitting the ball as cleanly as I would have hoped. I've had better days of hitting the ball, no question.

"It certainly becomes frustrating when your game is not anywhere near [the top] level. When you've been there and then all of a sudden your game is a little off, there's even more frustration involved."

Sampras thought Agassi's slump could be traced to the 1995 US Open final; hell, perhaps even to that 22-stroke rally that gave Sampras the first set.

"It's surprising," Sampras said, "because I think he's kind of like me in a way, in that he puts a lot of emphasis on the major titles and it seems like his mind really isn't where it should be. But I haven't talked to him in a while.

"We all know he has the talent to get it back. He just needs to get his mind straight and start working. It's been a little strange [to see him lose at the majors]; I find him one of the best guys out there."

Sampras continued, sounding like Ali without Frazier, saying, "I think Andre brings a lot to my game. He's made me a better player. He brings a lot to the game itself; he's a very popular player around the world and I think the game needs him [to do better]. He really brings a buzz to this tournament and that buzz has kind of gone because he's not here.

"It just goes to show that if you don't prepare well and you're not ready to go, you're not going to win."

Indeed, after Agassi lost, one British paper pulled no punches, declaring Wimbledon 'officially dead'.

And there was concern that as far as championships go, so too was Agassi.

"That shirt he wore made Andre Agassi look like Casper the Ghost," said commentator Bud Collins. "And right now, that's what Andre is in tennis — a ghost."

"It Was Always Wimbledon" 19

A CHANCE meeting intertwined the lives of Pete Sampras and his first coach, Pete Fischer. The story goes that Sampras' father, Sam, asked Fischer — a Los Angeles paediatrician and decent-enough club player — to hit with his nine-year-old son one afternoon at the Jack Kramer Tennis Club in Manhattan Beach.

A little later, Sam asked Fischer if he would hit with his son regularly. Sam said he'd pay. Fischer, astonished at the kid's ability, said no way. He'd do it for free. Thus began a player-coach relationship unique in origin and result.

Thus also began a pattern of admirable, unusual parental restraint.

Sam Sampras and his wife, Georgia, determined early on they would not meddle in the development of destiny. And they must have known, at some point, that their son was destiny personified.

Sam — Sotirios his given name — and Georgia. The father is American-born but of Greek descent, the mother a native of Sparta who emigrated to the United States. They met and married in Potomac, Maryland, where Pete was born.

Sam worked for the government — Department of Defense. He also owned a small restaurant. Silver spoons weren't available, for either customers or his four children.

The Samprases moved to Palos Verdes, California, in 1977. Life got better. Big surprise. Palos Verdes beats Potomac virtually any given day, in a variety of ways. Tennis is one of them.

As their son's tennis — which had its origin on the brick wall of a laundromat, with an old racquet he had found — improved, the parents fought the urge to watch. Sam had to fight harder. Georgia's instincts told her it was best to back off. In time, she convinced her husband of the same.

"Watching Pete play was wonderful," she told Eliot Berry, author of 1992's skillfully woven *Tough Draw*. "But having his parents as spectators was not the best thing for Pete."

This story has become classic: On the Sunday when their son was beating Agassi in the 1990 US Open final, Sam and Georgia, 3,000 miles away, went, well, shopping to pass the time and calm their nerves.

Strolling through a mall, they passed by a store with television sets blaring. The final, they saw on the screen, had finished. Their son clutched the winner's trophy. That's how they found out the kid had taken his first step toward fulfilling destiny. No big thing. After all, they had seen his real first steps. A much bigger deal.

Seldom have they wavered in their commitment to remain virtually invisible. And even when they have, deciding to witness first-hand the brilliance of their flesh and blood, there have been qualifiers.

They went to Palermo in the spring of 1995 to watch their son and Agassi pace a red-clay whitewash of the Italians in the second round of Davis Cup. They went out of their way to go unnoticed, even voicing those wishes to United States Tennis Association officials. Low profile. They wanted to trouble no one, wishing only to be left alone themselves.

"I also went to Moscow, for the Davis Cup final," Sam Sampras said. "That's been it."

"They were on my plane, to Palermo, and no one even knew it at first," said the USTA's Art Campbell. "And that's how they wanted it."

At Moscow, Sam "wanted very, very much to remain in the background."

Some symmetry there. As Georgia told Berry that she told Sam: "Let [Pete] alone; he does beautiful."

Tennis parents shunning attention. Now that is beautiful.

As is the most visible by-product of their restraint. Pete Sampras is his parents, through and through, in so many ways.

"I've known the family for years, been at their house, yet I've seen Georgia a total of, maybe, five times," said Winters. "Lovely lady, very old world; but she just doesn't have much of a hand in the tennis end of things.

"Sam? A pleasant man, but is much the same way [as his wife]. I wouldn't say there's not much to him, but it's just that there isn't very much public persona to him."

What top-ranked tennis player does that sound like?

Sam Sampras declined to discuss all this. "I just don't do interviews," he said, emphasising his point with 30 subsequent seconds of dead silence over the phone.

He added that he appreciated the chance to say no comment. He did so politely, directly, with no frills.

Kind of like his son's style.

Fischer was either a visionary or awfully lucky in making the snap assessment that Pete Sampras was something special. Looking over at what everyone else would call a little boy, Fischer saw a future Wimbledon champion.

"I knew [he could win it] from the first time I saw him," Fischer said.

Through the years, as Fischer mapped out his charge's development, the inkling of that first hit forever factored in. Goals formed as a result. And the first and foremost goal, Fischer determined, would be a Wimbledon title.

"It was always Wimbledon," Fischer said.

"Since time immemorial, Wimbledon has been the tournament that, by winning, players were considered the greatest in the world."

That overriding goal led Fischer to convince a 14-year-old Sampras to ditch his two-handed backhand in favour of a one-hander, to facilitate the serve-and-volley needed to win at you-know-where. Prior to the switch, Sampras was a fine junior player, a typical backcourt toiler, but one with undistinguished results, mainly because Fischer always had him 'play up' in an older age bracket. The emphasis was on development, not trophies. Also, lining up against older guys gave Sampras the chance to play pressure-free, to mould the free-swinging style that sets him apart today on the professional tour.

Mark Winters got to see much of Sampras' development first-hand, living and working the Southern California tennis scene. His early recollections of Sampras mirror Fischer's.

"I saw Pete first play when he was nine and my memories are very distinct," Winters said. "I referred to him back in those days as 'The Grin'. He had a mouthful of teeth. Also, he used to say the girls at school made fun of him because of his bushy eyebrows. And his body, it didn't quite fit the shot he had.

"Even back then, so extraordinary was his fluidity, his presence. But... how does a nine-year-old have presence? Watching Pete play, it was like going to look at new cars, seeing good ones, then seeing the best."

Except for, perhaps, one other, Fischer would add. Rod Laver became the standard of excellence by which to measure Sampras' every step, on and off the court. Laver went hand in hand with Wimbledon in the Fischer scheme. Fischer saw Sampras as a champion of the future, capable of renewing the past in a variety of ways. As Sampras matured, he left behind the odd tantrums of his youth, just as he did the two-handed backhand. Both stood in the way of progress.

"My whole game, my whole personality, changed when I changed my backhand," Sampras recalled. The Michael Chang-like grinder was replaced by a silky-smooth, instinctive player who painted serve-and-volley portraits and created stunning winners from the backcourt. Sampras had traded in his roller for an easel.

The court, once a cage, now was a canvas. And from there evolved a game with 1990s power but 1960s grace and purpose.

"He's got such a nice, flowing game," said Laver. "He's strong. He's accurate — damn accurate. And, he likes what he's doing."

Those years when it was gradually coming together for Sampras, looking back, seem to have been scripted by fate. How else to explain the hookup between a balding, middle-aged doctor with an appreciation for tennis tradition and a child who knew nothing except he loved to play?

"Fischer tried so hard to provide Pete with an understanding of the game, the importance of Rod Laver, the significance of those older guys," Winters said.

"And so, because of that, what we're seeing now, in Pete, is very rare: a true champion. Pete Sampras had a goal and Pete Fischer sculpted it.

"The goal was to be the consummate professional player."

A goal that could only be obtained by hoisting the Wimbledon trophy. Sampras was well-acquainted with that vision, long before he knew the feeling.

"My first real strong memory of Wimbledon was watching Becker win at the age of 17" Sampras said prior to the 1995 fortnight.

"I was like, 'God, that must be unbelievable to win that tournament.' You can't do anything more in tennis than win Wimbledon, so I've always put a lot of emphasis on it. It's the biggest event on the tour. I always put Wimbledon maybe one notch above the rest [of the majors] because of the history and the fact that it's the one tournament I always wanted to win. Hopefully I can win it as many times as I can.

"When you're a kid watching it on TV, you say, 'That's my goal, to be on Centre Court,' but you never really think it is going to come true. Then I got better and finally played my first Wimbledon when I was 17."

He lost in the first round, in four sets, to Todd Woodbridge. An inauspicious beginning, to say the least.

It would get worse before it got better.

But, as *Tennis* magazine's Pete Bodo wrote in his Wimbledon 1996 preview, 'Nobody ever found winning at Wimbledon easy.'

Sampras learned all about that, just as Pete Fischer knew he would, with time, despite several early stumbles that threw the championship timetable slightly askew.

"He's different," Fischer said. "He's Pete Sampras. He belongs on a tennis court."

Especially if the court is green, at Wimbledon.

Growing
Pains 20

NOBODY'S game is perfect. Not even Pete Sampras'. Most certainly, the Sampras who visited Wimbledon so hopeful in 1989-91 was an imperfect model. Grass made him look, initially, like a lemon.

But then, he was a hard-court boy through and through. During his junior days he rarely strayed from true-bounce security. Even clay courts were viewed with apprehension, despite a pre-teen game dependent on steady groundstroking.

Grass, even more of an unknown, was alluring. By the time he was 17, Sampras had the makings of a huge serve and was getting used to backing it up with volleys. Serve-and-volley; that's all he needed to win Wimbledon, right?

Uh-uh.

If one has a weapon, grass can turn it up a notch. Likewise, a problem area becomes magnified given the typical shortness of points. And man, did Sampras ever have a problem area.

In today's game, one shot has emerged as the key on grass courts. It's a shot you simply must master if you have championship desires. As Andre Agassi demonstrated in 1992, returning serves wins Wimbledons — or loses them.

Sampras' return stunk, to the point where he couldn't win

matches at Wimbledon. In his 1989 debut he lost to Woodbridge. The next year, flashy shot-maker Christo Van Rensburg gave him a straight-set lesson. In 1991, a milestone: Wimbledon victory No.1, over the legendary Danilo Marcelino. Solid grass-courter Derrick Rostagno eliminated Sampras in the next round.

Sampras won the US Open in 1990 with an obscene show of offence, but he couldn't cut it on the perfect surface for attackers. It puzzled the people who figured he'd slip comfortably into the grass-court game, people like Fred Perry, the great, three-time (1934-36) titlist who tabbed Sampras as a future champion.

At Wimbledon 1996, Sampras recalled Perry's prediction, joking about how it looked off-base.

"I heard Fred's comment and it was like, 'Wow, I've won one match in three years at Wimbledon; a man has to know his limitations'," Sampras said.

"But basically, when I first came to Wimbledon I couldn't return the first couple of years. I could serve well and hold my serve the majority of the time. I think over the years I've learned how to return a little better and how to pass and move, because I never really grew up playing on grass. It was pretty much hard-court tennis. I understand grass a little bit better and feel pretty good on it.

"I was surprised, though, that I didn't play too well my first three years."

Tim Gullikson wasn't. When he took over as Sampras' coach in 1992, he targeted the return, drawing upon his own success. Gullikson and his brother reached the Wimbledon doubles final. Another year, Gullikson upset McEnroe.

"You can't underestimate how important it was for Pete to change his return," Bodo said, "and Tim was incredibly good with the technical nuts and bolts of the game."

"Tim was such a good grass-court player, that I figured he could help me win Wimbledon," said Sampras.

Gullikson coaxed Sampras into playing percentages on his return, shortening his stroke slightly. His elongated swing pattern was too much, too late and seldom produced a threatening ball. What worked for Bjorn Borg in the 1970s would no longer fly, due to the increased power just about everyone possessed, power that mushroomed on grass.

Gullikson's concept borrowed from baseball, the art of fielding grounders: Play the ball, instead of letting the ball play you. The trick was attacking the serve in a controlled manner.

Gullikson also preached optimism in the face of aces, a grass-court fact of life that Sampras had trouble dealing with when he was on the receiving end. As Sampras' attitude improved, so did his tennis.

Wimbledon 1992 can be judged a breakthrough, even if Sampras did break down in a semi-final loss to Ivanisevic. A straight-set quarter-final victory over defending champion Michael Stich, with the loss of only nine games, stood as Sampras' Wimbledon highlight to that point. But against Ivanisevic he regressed, basically giving up, beaten down under a torrent of aces and service winners. He wasn't alone during the two weeks. Ivanisevic — who choked badly in losing the final to Agassi — bombed a tournament record 206 aces in his seven matches.

"That match was the one time that it got to the point where mentally I'd just had enough, where I just bailed out," Sampras told *Tennis* magazine.

"I had so little chance to return serves that I got really down on myself. I'm not sure people really understand how devastating that serve of his is. I'd step up to the line, not touch the ball, and be down love-30. Or I would work my butt off to get to 30 on his serve and then he'd pop two aces to even it out.

"It was overwhelming, that frustration."

Sampras set his mind to avoiding similar collapses in the future, especially against Ivanisevic, who he surely would meet again at Wimbledon. Having come so close to achieving his long-sought goal, Sampras yearned to make amends and perhaps, make history. Or at least be part of it.

Wimbledon, you see, had gotten to him. Just as Pete Fischer knew it would.

"It starts when you walk into the gate," Sampras said. "You really feel the character of the Centre Court and the character of the grounds. It is just different from any other Grand Slam tournament we play.

"It's the one that I always wanted to win as a little kid; hearing the echo of the ball on Centre Court, remembering Borg winning five times in a row, it's just always been pretty special to me."

The Run 21

NOW that Sampras finally had achieved contender status, it was time for the British press to sit up, take notice and attack. That's the memory of Sampras at Wimbledon 1993: under fire for his public persona, which was basically nil but was the same persona he'd always had.

No matter that he fulfilled his potential and levelled his half of the draw, with one truly tough match — a five-set quarter-final victory over defending champion Agassi — the only hindrance en route to the final against old Saddlebrook buddy Courier, who for once had found his form on grass courts.

Sampras won the final in four close sets, and awaited the acclaim that never came in a nation still wrapped up in Agassi, who had been named Britain's favourite sports personality in a recent poll. Sampras defeated Agassi in a five-set quarter-final, as Agassi's new acquaintance, actress Barbra Streisand, watched.

"How does it feel to be the most unpopular man at Wimbledon?" a British reporter asked Sampras afterward.

The first All-American final at the All-England Club since McEnroe defeated Connors in 1984 was dominated by Sampras' 22 aces and the partial disinterest of the Centre Court crowd.

Not counting Princess Diana, a solid supporter of Sampras throughout the nearly three-hour final. Sampras, informed of her backing, thought it very cool.

"Maybe she has a crush on me," he said.

Too bad the tabloids didn't. Their reports on the final stuck

Sampras with the laconic label that follows him to this day. The slams were across the board.

"It's Pete Samprazzzz; Bored on the Fourth of July," blared a *Daily Mirror* headline.

"Tennis is no longer sweet music," wrote a *Daily Telegraph* columnist. "Power has corrupted its spirit."

The morning-after attacks did two things. First, they robbed Sampras — and to a lesser extent, Courier — of recognition for a fortnight well done. Secondly, they set off a debate about Sampras' personality and the importance of personality, period, in determining tennis star quality

Sampras, who overcame a bad bout with tendinitis in his right shoulder, felt pressure like never before in this match, playing his long-time friend on a surface that favoured his game considerably.

"I liked my chances against Jim on grass," Sampras said. "It would have taken me maybe six months or a year to get over a Wimbledon final loss."

It had been almost three years since Sampras won his first major title, the 1990 US Open. As time passed, that looked more and more like a fluke.

It had been ten months since Sampras lost in the 1992 Open final to Stefan Edberg. That loss crushed Sampras, and stayed with him, really, until he converted his second match point against Courier. Finally, he was freed.

If he had lost to Courier, Sampras figures his career could have plunged. "The weight I put on myself was extreme," he told *The New York Times*. "I couldn't eat that day. I couldn't sleep the night before. The 1992 US Open taught me that nobody cares who the runner-up is."

Courier was going to school, dealing with a second consecutive major final setback. Several weeks earlier, he had failed to win a third consecutive French Open title, losing to Sergi Bruguera. On the upside, he had reached all three 1993 Grand Slam finals to date, starting the year with a victory at the Australian Open.

"I got outplayed," Courier said.

As did Boris Becker before him, in the semi-finals. And Agassi before that, to Barbra's dismay. Sampras had beaten the best, to win the biggest tournament and validate Pete Fischer's faith.

But for many, that wasn't enough. They wanted glitz with their groundstrokes. Sampras offered only excellence, in the tradition of the great players he held so dear. They came to his defence, as discussion of his style continued to resurface in the aftermath of Wimbledon 1993.

"It may be boring that people can't get his serve back, but don't call Pete boring," said his role model, Laver, who probably took the criticism of Sampras somewhat personally, and rightfully so.

"We should respect Pete's ability, and the fact that he's sharing that ability with us. Pete's gotten a bum rap, that he plays boring tennis."

"I don't go along with those people who say tennis needs more charisma," said Fred Stolle. "I've seen Pete become the No.1 player in the world and basically stay the same person.

"I don't want to embarrass myself out on the court," Sampras said. "I'm not really comfortable showing my emotions out there."

"I think Pete has a lot of facets to his personality," said journalist Sandra Harwitt. "A lot of these guys are kids when they come on the tour and I think a lot of times, people expect too much of them [beyond the tennis].

"A lot of people mistake Pete for being dull. I think he runs into the same image situation that Stefan Edberg always did. Stefan has a great, British-style dry humour. Pete is a little like that."

Sampras returned to Wimbledon in 1994 as the defending champion, with an absolute lock on the world No.1 ranking he had first achieved in April of 1993.

After winning his first Wimbledon title, he went on to take the 1993 US Open and 1994 Australian Open before losing in the French quarters to Courier. It had become quite apparent that like him or not, people had better get used to Pete Sampras.

Wimbledon came in the middle of a year when Sampras won a career-high ten titles and lost in the final of two other tournaments.

At year's end, despite an injury-hampered post-Wimbledon summer — he missed six tournaments with a bad ankle — he would become the first player to be No.1 for an entire year since Ivan Lendl in 1987, and first to win ten tournaments since Lendl in 1989.

Not bad for a boring guy.

Sampras now had four Grand Slam tournament titles. No longer merely talking the great Aussie tradition, but walking it.

"It makes all of us very proud to see a young man like Sampras recognising us," Stolle said. "Sampras is one of the very few players today who knows a lot about the history of the game."

"Those guys basically built the tour," Sampras said. "They deserve a lot of credit."

So did the 'gloomy robot' — that's what one British paper called Sampras in 1993 — for his ongoing construction project, including the Wimbledon phase. Sampras' early misgivings about grass courts "I thought it was an unfair surface," he said had been supplanted by a champion's confidence.

As evidenced in the first match of Wimbledon 1994.

Sampras and fellow Tampa resident Jared Palmer — his family operates the renowned Palmer Tennis Academy, a junior training mecca — had the honour of opening the tournament on Centre Court. Palmer, a former NCAA singles champion and one of the world's top doubles players, is a poor man's Sampras. His game is classic, even more stylish than Sampras. But he lacks the overall power, the one imposing weapon, needed to make the top ten. What Palmer does do is hit every ball very well, and he volleys better than almost anyone. On grass, that's enough to compete.

Sampras got through a first-set tie-breaker, then settled into a serving pattern that the British fans and the rest of the ATP Tour love to hate. Sampras aced the 56th-ranked Palmer 25 times — in only three sets.

"When I got into a rhythm like that, he really didn't have a clue where it was going," said Sampras.

Next morning, cursory positive reviews from the English press. But the *Daily Mirror* took another avenue to shoot Sampras down.

The paper ran a full-page photo spread on male pro players, all shirtless. Agassi, of course, was dubbed 'Sexy Seed 1'.

Sampras, of course, brought up the rear as 'Sexy Seed 7', with the explanation, 'Not the best of chests'.

Two more straight-set victories carried Sampras into the fourth round, but hardly anybody noticed. Circumstances had conspired from the outset of 'the Championships' to allow Sampras to go about his business of defending, unhindered by media attention.

On Day Two, top seed and defending champion Steffi Graf lost to Lori McNeil, opening the door for nine-time champion Martina Navratilova to make it ten in her Wimbledon swan song. With Graf gone, this would be Navratilova's tournament, until she lost.

Then a rash of upsets diverted attention. The 1991 champion Michael Stich lost to Bryan Shelton, who, like McNeil, is black. A torrent of blacks-at-Wimbledon stories ensued. Courier lost to Frenchman Guy Forget. Stefan Edberg, a fading, two-time champion, joined Courier on the second-round shelf, losing to Kenneth Carlsen.

Three-time champion Boris Becker kept winning but had to pay for it once. During a third-round victory over Javier Frana, Becker received massage treatment when he was supposed to be using the toilet. He was fined $1,000. Further allegations of gamesmanship, by several opponents, had Boris boiling.

Off-court silliness intervened, too. On a particularly windy day, Katrina Adams' tennis panties, a brightly coloured item known as 'Fancy Pants', became a hot-and-bothered topic. A day later, a British tabloid had one of its 'Page 3' topless girls wearing the same type of panties next to the headline 'Wimble-bum'.

Navratilova got Fleet Street charged up, by mentioning in a press conference that she had given thought to being a mother. Since Navratilova is gay, that started a rumble. Also, her entourage featured new companion Danda Jaroljmek plus a former one, pop singer k.d. Lang. Jaroljmek and Lang were photographed, arm in arm, walking the All-England Club grounds. The accompanying caption: 'Les be friends'.

Nothing like well-known lesbians to liven up Wimbledon.

Sampras? Almost an afterthought.

After his Centre Court opener, he was banished to the smaller stadiums at Court 1 and Court 2 for victories over Richey Reneberg, Chuck Adams and Daniel Vacek. That pretty much said it all, regarding the champion's image.

But image is not everything. After beating Michael Chang in a quarter-final, Sampras had yet to lose a set in five matches, with cumulative court time of just over seven hours.

For the semi-finals, Sampras — returned to Centre Court — expected a longer stay. His opponent, Todd Martin, had fought hard in losing the Australian Open final, then harder in beating Sampras one week before Wimbledon in the Queen's Club final.

"I'd say I'm not going through those peaks and valleys I was going through [at Queen's Club]," Sampras said.

"You probably get up for Wimbledon more. I'm not saying I didn't try to win at Queen's, but Wimbledon is the biggest tournament we have."

Sampras-Martin. No.1 and No.6 seeds, 1-2 in the decorum rankings, with Martin in front. Martin is perhaps the only person on tour more polite — some would say more boring, granted — than Sampras. The Brits deserved this, a double-dose of decorum, an afternoon of short, serving-dominated points with nary a word spoken by the participants.

Sampras won, but a revelation — he dropped a set. Martin won the third set, taking three consecutive games from 3-3 after Sampras slightly twisted his right ankle as he fell while hitting a running forehand. His right foot scraped into the grass that now was greenish brown, digging a rut.

"I was a little bit stunned because I did feel a very minor twist," Sampras said. "But I just walked it out and it didn't bother me the rest of the match. I may just tape it up [for the final]."

"When Pete's in the lead he plays better; I need to acquire that trait," Martin said.

In the other semi, Goran Ivanisevic continued his shooting-gallery style of tennis that is far more boring than Sampras'. Ivanisevic is a one-dimensional player, but at Wimbledon, if that one-dimension is serving, you're in business.

In straight-setting Becker, Ivanisevic cranked the fortnight's fastest serve, 136mph. He had 22 aces, boosting his tournament total to 140. Some unusual brilliant backcourt play led to the match-deciding service breaks.

Sampras now had his chance to complete his Wimbledon evolution, his competitive evolution, really. The 1992 semi-final loss to Ivanisevic stunted both growth patterns.

Ivanisevic came in with a 5-3 career edge on Sampras, talking as big as he serves.

"Pete doesn't like to play me," Ivanisevic said. "Pete can also beat me easy, but he doesn't like the lefty serve on grass. He always has a problem with lefties."

After that reasonable offering, Ivanisevic came up with some strange stuff, leading believers to think he'd been playing a different tournament the previous 13 days.

"Pete's very confident at the moment, but he's not unbeatable. I saw him against Martin and he's also a human being. He can make mistakes."

Sampras' counter:

"I feel if I play my best or play well, I'm pretty tough to beat. I think I do everything well. I return well, serve well."

The final between the two huge servers faltered again, for those longing for backcourt rallies. But the intrigue was undeniable. Neither player could break serve during the first two sets, but Sampras claimed both in tie-breakers. At that point, Ivanisevic's desire snapped. He went down 6-0 in the last set.

You had to hate the love-set. A miserable effort and unfortunate footnote to Wimbledon 1994, a tournament still peaking from the women's final the day before when Conchita Martinez ended Navratilova's dream run with a three-set victory.

"You lose two sets 7-6 and it puts pressure on you," Ivanisevic said. "And I had to keep at my best. If you miss some first serves

THE EARLY YEARS

(Left) After the switch. Sampras gets ready to try his new one-handed slice backhand during the summer before his first US Open in 1988.

(Left) Pete Sampras has tried to emulate the classic style of Rod Laver (pictured) and other great Australian players from previous eras.

(Right) Sixteen-year-old Pete Sampras with (from left to right) his father, Sam; his first coach, Pete Fischer; and his brother Gus.

RIVALRIES

(Far left) Two great serve-and-volleyers, Sampras and Boris Becker, stand at the net before their 1995 Wimbledon final. (Left) Sampras and Michael Chang have been rivals since 1980, when they met in a boys' 10-and-under tournament championship. Chang was the stronger then, but not in 1997.

(Far left) Jim Courier greets Sampras with a wide smile at the 1995 US Open. Pete beat him in four tough sets. (Left) Sampras and Andre Agassi share one of the most publicised rivalries in tennis — but not quite in this moment!

WIMBLEDON 1995

(Above) Showing his backcourt mobility, Sampras gets ready for a baseline backhand during Wimbledon.

(Above) Sampras throws his shirt into the stands to celebrate his win in the final.

(Left) Sampras raises the Wimbledon trophy in 1995 after winning the championship for the third consecutive year. His victory was 'a little bit more of a struggle' than his two previous Wimbledon victories.

US OPEN 1995

(Above) Fielding questions from reporters: How does it feel to have John F. Kennedy Jr. and Arnold Schwarzenegger in the stands?

(Right) Celebration time. Sampras salutes the crowd after his 1995 US Open triumph.

(Left) During the Sampras-Agassi final on Sunday, the wind made things difficult, often favouring the man hitting into it.

(Right) Delaina Mulcahy (first row, middle) watches Sampras defeat Agassi in the final.

DAVIS CUP 1995

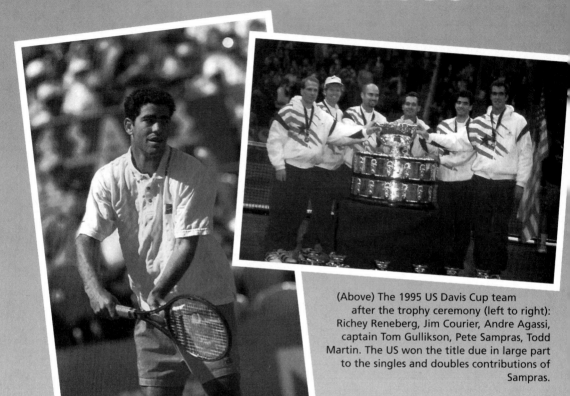

(Above) The 1995 US Davis Cup team after the trophy ceremony (left to right): Richey Reneberg, Jim Courier, Andre Agassi, captain Tom Gullikson, Pete Sampras, Todd Martin. The US won the title due in large part to the singles and doubles contributions of Sampras.

(Above) Sampras delivering one of the serves that helped his Davis Cup reputation come full circle during three days of clutch tennis against Russia in the 1995 final.

AUSTRALIAN OPEN 1996

(Right) In the 1996 Australian Open, despite powerful forehands like this one, Sampras lost in three straight sets to Mark Philippoussis in the third round.

FRENCH OPEN 1996

(Left) Sampras played under a shadow during the 1996 French Open — his first tournament since his coach, Tim Gullikson, lost his battle against cancer.

(Right) Sampras reached the semi-finals by playing the clay-court tournament "on my terms".

US OPEN 1996

(Above) Sampras fights an attack of stomach cramps from dehydration during his remarkable quarter-final win over Corretja.

(Above) The Sampras-Corretja five-setter left the two with just enough strength for an embrace.
(Right) Getting to be a habit. Sampras cradles the trophy symbolic of his 1996 victory in the US Open.

REFLECTIONS

(Below) At Wimbledon in 1996. Rain delays did not help Sampras' concentration as he lost in the quarter-final to Richard Krajicek, the eventual winner.

(Above) When Sampras was in his mid-teens, Pete Fischer, Sampras' first coach, supervised the pivotal Sampras switch from a two-handed to a one-handed backhand.

(Below) Coach Tim Gullikson with Sampras at practice during the 1994 French Open. Gullikson's death in May 1996 had a significant impact on Sampras.

Pete Sampras in defiant mood during the ATP World Championship final in Germany, November 1996.

Pete Sampras during Wimbledon, 1996.

or easy volleys, you're gone. As soon as he broke me the first time [in the third set] it was sufficient."

The third set lasted 19 minutes and with the Wimbledon title on the line, Ivanisevic's performance was, to say the very least, disappointing in the extreme. He let down himself, the fans and Sampras.

"His serve probably came in about 10mph slower in the third set," Sampras said. "He just got really down on himself and that's when I raised my tennis a notch. And that's why it came out 6-0 in the third. I really couldn't play any better."

"Today, Pete was just too good," Ivanisevic conceded.

For once, Wimbledon fans seemed to agree. After the match, before the trophy presentations, both players tossed their racquets and sweat-soaked shirts into the stands. Moments later, as Sampras paraded around Centre Court, the crowd cheered loudly.

"I think I'm winning their hearts," Sampras said. "But my main concern is to win [matches]. I just hope people can appreciate how I go about my tennis. People can write what they want and when they want, but the fact is I've got two Wimbledons in a row and that's going to stay with me."

Unfortunately, so would that ankle injury. From Wimbledon, Sampras headed to The Netherlands to play Davis Cup, on hard courts. The ankle couldn't take the pounding, and a tendinitis situation developed, forcing Sampras to withdraw from six tournaments and, in effect, leading to his early exit from the US Open.

The fact that he found his Wimbledon form, for the second consecutive year, eases that painful memory.

Wimbledon was an especially welcome sight in June 1995. Things had to get better at some point, and maybe this would be the place. Sampras hoped so.

It had been six months after Gullikson's cancer diagnosis. It had been three weeks since Sampras' first-round French Open loss, after which he found himself at an all-time low, even though the rankings said he still was the world's No.2-ranked player, behind Agassi.

"I had just lost in the French and I came back home to Tampa, walked in the door and dropped my bags down and just felt so depressed," Sampras said. "That was the first time in my life I could ever remember feeling like that. I was down. The year wasn't going well. At that point it really seemed like it was all rolling downhill. Losing in the Australian final, dealing with Tim's situation, not playing well on the clay…

"For so many years my life had been so organised. Then, suddenly I was having to deal with a good friend's life [possibly ending]. The first two or three months after [the diagnosis] were really tough emotionally because no one really knew what was going on or how serious it was. Now he's in treatment and doing really well and hopefully he can get back to travelling. But obviously his health is the most important thing right now. I'm just trying to give him all the support I can."

Gullikson, limited to coaching by phone — "We talk three or four times a week about my tennis and about life in general," Sampras said — was in tune with Sampras' state of mind.

Somehow, he talked Sampras out of it. Just in time for Wimbledon.

"Tim just said I needed to go to Wimbledon with a new attitude," Sampras recalled. "His attitude was that I did well at the Australian by making the final, didn't do well at the French but that I had two more chances — Wimbledon and the US Open — to save my year.

"How ironic it was. Tim's fighting for his life, but he had a better attitude than I did."

Something clicked. Sampras flew to London, and he won both singles and doubles at Queen's Club. Todd Martin was his partner, in the rare doubles appearance.

"I got a whole new start at Queen's," Sampras said.

His Wimbledon start was new. And different. Sampras drew 120th-ranked Karsten Braasch, the man of a thousand spins, an athlete who smokes — he used to light up during changeovers — and drinks and never hits the same shot twice in a row.

"He's a pain to play," Sampras said with a smirk, after a four-set victory that started with a split of tie-breakers, the second going to Braasch.

"After losing the second set I wasn't a very happy camper. I needed to regain my composure. I didn't get a rhythm until I broke him in the third."

Composure and rhythm still were lacking in a three-set, second-round victory over British hopeful Tim Henman and a rematch with Jared Palmer in the third round, requiring four sets. At least it appeared that way, possibly because Sampras' performances will forever be measured against the standards of 1994.

The price of excellence.

"Yeah, if I lose a set to someone, all of a sudden everybody thinks I'm so vulnerable," he said. "But I could lose a set to my mother on grass."

Well, maybe to his sister, Stella, a 1988 NCAA doubles champion and UCLA coach. But Sampras' absurdity made a valid point. Grass is the great equaliser, even if the world's best player is involved.

"I didn't get off to a great start [against Palmer]," he said, "but I think my form throughout the tournament can get better. This is kind of where I want to be at the moment, playing pretty well. But there's definitely room to get better."

And a perfect time to start, in a fourth-round match against Greg Rusedski, who also trained at Saddlebrook and occasionally hit with Sampras when both were around. Rusedski, the game's fastest server, had won over the Wimbledon crowds with only three victories, since he now was a Brit. A Canadian by birth but long-time holder of a British passport — his mother is British — Rusedski recently had declared himself eligible for the British Davis Cup team; as the world's 60th-ranked player he immediately became his adopted country's No.1. The fact that he made the switch right before Wimbledon looked calculated, obviously.

Then Rusedski came to Wimbledon and tried his best to act

English. Little phrases — 'telly', for instance — started creeping into his speech. After one victory on Centre Court, he pulled off his Union Jack headband and started waving it, inciting the crowd. Meanwhile, the tabloids ate it up. One would have thought Rusedski had won two Wimbledons, instead of the man he was about to face.

Rusedski was a less-than-popular guy in the locker room during the tournament. Seems everyone got tired, quick, of hearing about him. Given a chance to end the hype, Sampras did so in three sets. He then fired a few more shots Rusedski's way, calling him 'pretty average' except for his serve and noting that "he has a couple of holes in his game, some things he needs to improve."

"I felt I had a lot of chances but Pete took most of the important points," Rusedski said. "I guess that's why he's been No.1 in the world and has won this tournament two years straight."

Into the quarter-finals, Sampras had again benefited from other happenings that took the press away and the pressure off.

Andre Agassi was advancing nicely, always welcomed at Wimbledon, as 'Agassi kits' were passed out to kids, complete with bandanas, earrings and goatees. Boris Becker looked tough and hadn't annoyed anyone yet, which was big news. On the women's side, Chanda Rubin defeated Patricia Hy-Boulais in the longest women's match in tournament history, 58 games.

And what about Jeff Tarango?

On the tournament's first Saturday, Tarango quit during a match because of a line-call dispute, and he called chair umpire Bruno Rebeuh 'the most corrupt official in the game'. Tarango headed to a post-match interview where he alleged that Rebeuh had a history of helping certain players win matches. Rebeuh also met up with Mrs. Tarango, a fiery French woman named Benedicte. She slapped Rebeuh, then attended the interview, where she kept intervening. A total of $15,500 in fines and a one-year ban from Wimbledon resulted.

Sampras' quarter-final found him against another Saddlebrook client, Japan's top player, Shuzo Matsuoka. A match with an interesting sidelight: Matsuoka's coach at the time was Alvaro Betancur; many times, when Sampras trains at Saddlebrook, guess whom he hits with? That's right, Betancur. Sampras and Matsuoka have also practised together.

Betancur must have known something about Sampras' game, because Matsuoka won the first set in a tie-breaker and had three break points for a 4–3 second-set lead, before Sampras escaped, en route to a four-set victory. Afterward, Betancur wouldn't comment on the inside information theory. Later, he explained that he didn't want to anger Sampras.

Another meeting with Goran Ivanisevic, in the semi-finals, proved far more competitive that the 1994 final, as competitive as possible, with Sampras winning one more point — 146–145 — overall, in a five-set victory.

More sets meant more aces: 38 for Ivanisevic, 21 from Sampras. The best illustration of the match's high quality was first-serve percentage: 63 per cent for Sampras, 61 for Ivanisevic.

A wonderfully contested affair, but leave it to Ivanisevic to ruin a good thing. In what has since become a regular refrain, he blamed the loss on being 'unlucky'. Other than a Sampras volley that trickled over the net on break point in the first set, luck seemed to take this match off, but Ivanisevic saw it differently.

"Every time I had a break point, I hit a good shot and he had some luck," Ivanisevic said. "I don't know... a mis-hit or something."

This match resembled the 1992 semi-final between the two, with one exception. This time, Sampras waited Ivanisevic out, accepting the aces with the errors, figuring it would all shake out his way in the long run.

"When you're playing Goran it's kind of like a roller-coaster," Sampras said. "A scary roller-coaster. He has, by far, the biggest serve in the game, maybe in the history of the game. I just tried to get it back as much as possible and not get too discouraged about him hitting two or three aces a game."

After winning, Sampras sat back and awaited the outcome of the other semi between Agassi and Becker, expecting his partner-in-shoe-sales to come through. Agassi had a five-year, eight-match victory streak going against Becker. When he went up a set and 4-1 — with two second-set service breaks — the dream final, the ultimate renewal of 'The Rivalry of the 1990s', seemed certain.

Then, Becker suddenly changed tactics. A slight adjustment, as he started trading with Agassi from the baseline a bit more, abandoning his strategy of attacking constantly. Becker began picking and choosing his forays to the net. Agassi's shots, more often than not, started finding the net.

Becker came back to take the second set in a tie-breaker, dropping only one point. He then ran out the match, winning the last two sets 6-4, 7-6, again losing only one point in the second tie-breaker.

"I just thought giving him a target [at the net] all the time was something Andre likes very much," Becker said. "I don't think I have ever run that much on a grass court in my life. I felt like, sure, he's going to be a little bit better than me from the baseline, but I'm still going to be able to play with him."

"Everything was right on schedule until that lead slipped away," Agassi said. "I felt like I deserved to be up two sets. Then he got away and by the time all was said and done he picked up his level and I never managed to pick up mine."

In lieu of Agassi, Becker would do nicely for the Centre Court crowd in the final. He had won his first title there 11 years earlier, at the age of 17, forever cementing his popularity with fans. As he went on to win twice more, he came to talk of Centre Court as his backyard. "It's where I grew up," he said. Eventually, he was more or less embraced by all, and his kinship with Wimbledon took on a Borg-like mystique.

In 1995, when he outlasted Cedric Pioline in a four-hour, five-set quarter-final 9-7 in the fifth — the magic was back, and it stayed around to engulf Agassi.

"Even when I'm down I have a chance [at Wimbledon]," Becker said. "Nobody should underestimate me at Wimbledon."

Sampras wouldn't. His respect for tennis history helped. He recognised that Becker, in some ways, remained the people's champion of Wimbledon even though he hadn't won the tournament since 1989. Becker — who hadn't reached a Grand Slam tournament final since 1991, the year he was the world's No.1-ranked player — was the man who ended the previous era, that of John McEnroe and Jimmy Connors.

By defeating Becker in the final, Sampras could provide another closure, truly making Wimbledon his own. He also could convince people, again, that he truly belonged among the All-England elite. Sampras' 1994 tournament had spoiled people. In 1995 when he lost sets to Braasch, Palmer and Matsuoka, Wimbledon obituaries were prepared.

"I still feel like I'm pretty tough on grass," Sampras said after his semi-final. "Whereas last year everything was going so smoothly, I was playing the right guys at the time [and winning easily], this year it's been a little bit more of a struggle. But I've still been winning."

Becker announced, after beating Agassi, that his game was "better than ten years ago; if I would have had to play as many shots from the backcourt [then] I couldn't have done it. I didn't have the strokes and I didn't have the legs. I'm still serving and volleying and I'm still able to hang in there when I'm down.

"What does this mean to me? What can I say?"

Sampras could say this, when asked about his desire for a third title: "I'm ravenous."

Becker's comeback: "It seems like two hungry boys are going to play."

Hunger and desire, though, had no effect on the final, a match showcasing two great players while showing how much tennis had changed since Becker burst on the scene to preview the power game that now has passed him by.

Becker played well. Sampras played better: a 23-16 ace advantage, an 88-68 margin in winners. A 6-7 6-2, 6-4, 6-2 victory in which Sampras never faced a break point.

"When Pete's really feeling good about his serve he actually goes for both serves," Becker said. "That was the trouble. I didn't have a normal return to hit.

"It's a completely different game now than it was [ten years ago] and I'm glad I've managed to play both [eras]. To experience that is something I'm going to tell my kids about."

Becker may not reach another Wimbledon final, a fact lost on neither him nor the Centre Court patrons. Perhaps sensing this could be his last appearance in a post-final ceremony, Becker seized the moment from the champion. A consolation prize.

Becker gave a quick, playful wave to Princess Diana in the Royal Box. Then, after Sampras walked around holding his trophy aloft, Becker responded to the crowd's urgings and did a quick lap around the court with his smallish runner-up plate. Unprecedented for a loser.

A touching scene, surely. But for Sampras and his supporters there was reason to seethe, so great was the inequity in applause. Sampras' ovation was limited and polite. It should have been outrageous.

The crowd had been blinded by Becker, oblivious to the moment, to a wonderful story that unfolded before their clouded view.

If only they had watched. Really watched. More so, if only they had listened, they would have heard the single, solitary voice, audible during those moments between points, urging Sampras on by triggering something deep within his being.

But then, even for those who did hear it, it probably didn't seem like much.

"C'mon, Pistol."

For Sampras, it was everything.

The voice originated from a Gullikson. Not the stricken one, but the twin brother Tom, who sat behind the guest box overlooking one end of Centre Court. His urgings split the silence, shot across the stadium and found their mark.

Poor Becker. With the greatest player in the world getting this sort of encouragement, he had no chance.

"It sounded just like Tim," Sampras said softly after the match, after a phone call to Tim, back home in Illinois.

"Tom is a great friend and obviously we have both dealt with Tim's situation in a very public way. Tom's been hanging out for the last couple of weeks and has helped me out with my tennis. But just to have him here, to have that support, really felt good out on the court. When I heard 'Pistol,' I knew it was him."

"I'm not sure when Pete got that nickname," Tom said. "But he certainly pulled the trigger."

So many emotions, all around. So much graciousness, on both sides, especially Becker's.

"It's an amazing feat, what Pete has done," Becker said. "I watched his matches last year and it seemed real easy, if you can ever call a Wimbledon victory easy. But this year he had to struggle. He wasn't playing as well and had to come back in many matches. To be able to pull it off is something really, really special."

Sampras, fittingly, said he had "dedicated this win to Tim because he's a true champion. The way he's handled his treatment is just an inspiration. I talked to him after every match. He gave me the encouragement to go on after losing at the French Open and to win a 'Three-Pete' for him."

Later in 1995, after going on to win a third US Open and leading the United States to the Davis Cup, Sampras looked back and called Wimbledon the catalyst.

"Wimbledon saved my year," Sampras said. "Looking back, I remember thinking during the final 'I'm making history here' by winning a third straight time."

The vanquished Becker said it best.

"I used to own Centre Court... but it belongs to Pete now."

Dutch Treatment 22

S AMPRAS followed the Agassi plan, readying for Wimble-don 1996. Avoid the grass until you have to, is the Agassi philosophy.

"He's about the only player who just comes over and gets by on his talent," Sampras marvelled.

Never has Sampras gone into a Wimbledon with less grass-court practice. It showed in his first match, against Reneberg. Though Sampras escaped in four sets, he lost the first set and nearly dropped the second, down a service break.

Reneberg returned superbly early on, testimony to his steady doubles efforts on the tour. The fact that he and Sampras have practised together frequently the last few years, as members of the US Davis Cup team, also figured in.

"He knew what I was going to do and vice versa," Sampras said, admitting some misgivings over his limited grass-court preparation.

"It was not an easy match to play, not having played a match in a while. Richey is a good all-around player, and it was my first match on grass since last year [in the final]. I was a little bit slow at the beginning. He was returning my second serve like it was nothing. He kept on hitting winners right and left. He's got one of the best returns I've ever played against.

"I told myself I wasn't going to panic [when he won the first set] but I was getting a little bit panicked when he broke me in the second; the way he was returning and playing I was getting a little bit concerned at that point. But I broke back, and I think as the match wore on and I finally settled down, I started playing really well."

Well, sort of. Certainly he would need a sterner effort against Philippoussis, who overpowered Javier Frana in his first-round match.

This frightening early-round test had Sampras joking nervously. "I don't know what I've done to deserve this, but it's just the way the draw goes," he said. "You have to just go out and play."

Sampras loves to make statements, even if he doesn't admit to it. Revenge revs him up. If it happens at major tournaments, all the better. Nothing like putting guys back in their place, with the world watching. Yzaga, US Open 1995; Rusedski, Wimbledon 1995; Ivanisevic, Wimbledon 1994, just three examples.

Philippoussis potentially was another. Accordingly, Sampras oozed motivation as they walked on to Centre Court — Philippoussis' first such walk — on Wimbledon's fourth day.

"I've always looked at whenever you lose to someone, you always look forward to playing him again," Sampras said. "When I saw the draw, this was a match I looked forward to in some ways. In other ways, he's very dangerous with the way he serves; it's almost like he's hitting two first serves. He just goes for it. He takes a huge cut on his returns and passing shots and if he hits a couple of clean winners to break you then there's nothing you can do but hang in there and be patient on his serve and hopefully get a chance to break him."

Sampras got seven chances, converting two, all he needed to post a straight sets win since he never faced a break point.

"Not a lot of strategy out there," he said.

The numbers bore him out. Philippoussis averaged 122mph on his first serve, 111 on his second; Sampras averaged 117 and 100.

Philippoussis out-aced Sampras 28-15 but was out-of-sorts at times, trying to field Sampras' shrewdly-placed returns.

"I think aces mean nothing," Philippoussis said, a strange statement considering his current reliance on them.

"I would prefer to serve no aces and win the match than serve 500 aces and lose the match. I think you're better to get consistency with the first serve than aces. And first serves and first volleys are more important than smacking away on the serve, but I'm still young and I'm sure I'll learn that as I get on."

Philippoussis noticed Sampras' fire.

"I think this was much different [than the Australian Open]," Philippoussis said. "I think Pete was definitely more determined for revenge, to let everyone know that maybe the last time I beat him was a fluke or something. Strangely enough, I think I was more nervous out there on Centre Court than back at home in front of my crowd."

"The way Mark played in Australia was phenomenal," Sampras said. "Basically he kind of destroyed me, and played with a lot of confidence. That was on Rebound Ace [hard court] and this was grass and it was different tennis. We played a lot more from the backcourt in Australia and this match was much more serving. The difference was I just played a little better on the big points, returned a little better. But it was just a matter of trying to get his serve back and him trying to return mine."

Small difference. Big ramification. Wimbledon was the third meeting between Sampras and Philippoussis, all in Grand Slam tournaments. Consensus is that they'll meet again in Slams, possibly in finals. By winning now, Sampras establishes an edge he might draw upon down the road.

In winning this particular time, he took Philippoussis to Grand Slam school.

"I think I've just got to learn to be a lot tougher," Philippoussis said. "A guy like Pete doesn't give you any free points. He makes you work hard for everything and I think that's what I have to try to learn, not to give away any free points."

"I don't know if you'd want to call this a lesson," Sampras said. "I just felt like I'd been on Centre Court a lot more and it's a court I'm very comfortable on. But it was really pretty simple. I just won the bigger points."

Whatever questions existed about Sampras' winning the tournament dissipated with the dismissal of Philippoussis. It may have been Sampras' best Wimbledon match since the 1994 final, considering the opponent.

Then appeared the imposing figure of Karol Kucera, a steady but nondescript Slovak who hung around long enough to be the recipient of a rare Sampras choke-job.

Sampras took the first two sets then stumbled into a third-set tie-break that he let slip away (7-5) after missing a wide-open backhand volley. Extended to another tie-break, Sampras survived (7-3) against an opponent he was playing for the first time. Cool, windy conditions made it a tough serving day, a tough day all around.

"My form didn't seem as good as it has been the first couple of rounds," Sampras said, "but I got through it. It wasn't pretty. Just one of those matches where you want to get through and stick around."

Tougher matches were ahead, but it had started to look like the final might be anticlimactic. The bottom half of the draw, opposite Sampras, that lost Agassi on opening day also had lost No.2 seed Boris Becker, who severely strained his wrist while playing qualifier Neville Godwin in a third-round match.

"There are still a lot of great players playing and I'm still around," Sampras said, "so I'll just worry about who I'm playing, what I'm trying to achieve and playing my tennis."

Cedric Pioline, who pushed Becker all over Centre Court in a valiant 1995 loss, wasn't up to a repeat, in a fourth-round match against Sampras, again on Centre, that was delayed a full day because of the rain starting to take Wimbledon over.

Sampras lost eight games to the 16th-seeded Frenchman, forgot about Philippoussis and declared the match his best of the fortnight.

"I returned about as well as I could," he said. "I didn't serve that great [52 per cent of first serves] but it was a really solid perform- ance. Cedric's a very talented player. Grass isn't his best surface but he came pretty close to beating Boris here last year, so to go out and beat him pretty convincingly made me happy."

Sampras' toughest moment of the Pioline match: Midway through the second set, he chased a short Pioline shot and couldn't stop his momentum, which was taking him directly toward a chair at the sideline. On the run, Sampras leaped over the chair and landed on the large container used to hold tennis balls.

"I had only one place to go and that was up, over the chair and landed on the ball... whatever you call it," Sampras said. "It kind of tweaked my back a little bit but it's not too bad. A little bit scary situation there, though.

"It was like 'Holy shit', I was looking for some land."

Sampras won 11 consecutive points after that.

"Guess it wasn't too bad, then," he said.

"I've been waiting on Richard Krajicek for years," John McEnroe, now a television commentator, said on the eve of the men's quarter-finals.

He wasn't alone.

Krajicek, a 6ft 5ins Dutchman with one of the biggest serves in the world — he started 1996 with a career-best of 134mph, third fastest of all time — had carved a quick niche in his five previous Wimbledons, as one of the modern era's biggest grass-court busts.

From 1991-95 he never made it past the fourth round, with that high-water mark coming once, in 1993. In 1994 and 1995 he exited in the first round, the ultimate indignity for an alleged contender. In 1996, Wimbledon's seeding committee passed judgment in their own inimitable way. Despite a No.13 world ranking, Krajicek was excluded from the seedings, although when original No.7 Thomas Muster withdrew with an injury, the committee declared Krajicek an unofficial 17th seed and moved him into Muster's place on the bracket sheet.

Krajicek was known for other things besides Wimbledon

failure. A Wimbledon press conference mainly. In 1992 the subject of women's professional tennis came up and Krajicek commented that most women pros were 'lazy, fat pigs'.

He also had a knack for getting injured. Andre Agassi nailed him on that, after his third-round retirement from the Australian Open, saying all Krajicek had to do was 'look at a tennis court' to get hurt.

Your basic under-achiever. A good three-word summation for the 24-year-old from Rotterdam, coming into Wimbledon with a 27-16 1996 record with his best results, oddly, coming on slow red clay — finalist at the Italian Open, quarter-finals at the French Open.

But there was something there. Sampras would vouch for that, as he prepared to meet Krajicek in the quarters. He and the Dutchman had split four previous matches.

First meeting at Wimbledon, though, which Sampras wanted to emphasise, throwing in a reminder of the Centre Court factor, always a good idea.

"I feel that someone is going to have to outplay me," he said. "I'm playing well, I'm very comfortable on that court and I've been out there many times over the past three or four years. It's going to take someone to play well to beat me.

Krajicek qualified. Through four matches he had 89 aces and 64 per cent first-serve success, unusually high numbers when considered together. In a second-round victory against Derrick Rostagno, Krajicek achieved 20 aces and no double-faults. In a fourth-round upset of the 1991 champion, Michael Stich, he won 88 per cent of his first-service points even though his total of aces dropped to 13.

Sampras-like numbers there, completing Krajicek's fortnight transformation into Euro-Sampras. After all, Krajicek also abandoned a two-handed backhand during his junior days. He also likes golf and loves the Los Angeles Lakers. He too idolises one of the game's past greats, McEnroe. And finally, his girlfriend Daphne Deckers, a Netherlands television star, like Delaina Mulcahy, could turn heads. Clothing was a dead heat. The two Nike endorsers wore identical outfits.

Their match, by all rights, should have been the highlight of Wimbledon, what with the depleted bottom half of the draw that seemed destined to deliver an unseeded player to the final or, at best, the 13th-seeded Todd Martin. During Wimbledon's second week, though, rain dictated the order of play and affected the quality of it, unquestionably.

Sampras and Krajicek came out on Wimbledon's second Wednesday, 30 minutes late due to the tournament's heaviest rain. They split four games, with Sampras already letting six break points escape his usual vice-like grip, before the skies opened again.

A three-hour and 30-minute delay ensued during which Wimbledon entertained itself. Over on Court 1, members of the British armed forces who were serving as volunteer ushers led the crowd in songs and games of charades. The real show, though, developed on Centre Court where veteran pop star Sir Cliff Richard appeared near the rear of the Royal Box with a wireless microphone and started singing an a cappella medley of his hits, inviting spectators to join in the spontaneous concert. Behind him, a group of players past and present filed in to dance and sing back-up, including former champions Virginia Wade, Conchita Martinez, Pam Shriver and Gigi Fernandez — and finally, to a loud ovation, Martina Navratilova. Sir Cliff called them his 'Supremes'.

As the singer closed down his set — "I never thought I'd be playing Centre Court," he told the crowd — the rain stopped and the sun reappeared, as if on cue. It had been a delightful interlude in a dismal day that soon turned even more dismal for Sampras.

Sampras, having sat and steamed about the lost break-point chances, got no more for the balance of the set. Krajicek was cranking now, going up 6-5 with his 100th and 101st aces of the tournament.

Sampras, though, went through five service games without allowing any break points; but on his sixth service his head spun as Krajicek lashed a forehand crosscourt winner, then a backhand down the line to make it love-40. Sampras got his first serve in, but Krajicek nailed another forehand winner, a down-the-line pass, to ice the set.

Sampras had lost first sets before, but this did not look good. He didn't look good, showing signs of his old defeatist gait — the kind he slipped into against Kafelnikov at the French — even though it was still early in the match.

They started the second set by staying on serve through three games. After Krajicek held for 2-1 the rain returned, forcing a second interuption, lasting an hour and 40 minutes. Upon resumption, services were held through 6-6 with Sampras saving one set point serving at 5-6, with a backhand volley winner that Krajicek argued was out.

On to the tie-breaker, and into a five-point run by Krajicek that featured two aces, a brilliant backhand passing shot and a Sampras double-fault. Sampras came back to 5-3, but then missed his signature groundstroke — the running forehand — wide, giving Krajicek a set point at 6-3.

Sampras served and tried to volley. But he had no chance at coming close to yet another backhand return down the line. Set to Krajicek.

After a split of two games came yet another rain delay — plus one of the most bizarre incidents in the event's 110 years.

Ground crews, highly trained to cover courts at breakneck speed, raced on to Centre Court, lined up and started their well-rehearsed ritual of running backward while pulling the tarpaulin across the grass. One crew member slipped down. Per procedure — procedure is everything at Wimbledon, even when it comes to lawn maintenance — the covering continued, with the fallen crew member required to crawl from underneath and continue with the duty of helping secure the tarp.

But Mark Hillaby wasn't moving, as shown by the unsightly bump under the tarp. As the crowd hushed, the crew went back in the other direction with the cover, exposing the fallen Hillaby, who weakly motioned with one hand that he needed help.

He had hit his head, he said, on one of the heavy metal clips used to attach the tarp at courtside. Hillaby, removed from Centre Court on a stretcher, was taken to a nearby hospital, examined and released.

During the wait for the stretcher, a light rain soaked Centre Court, which was half exposed due to the accident to Hillaby. And so, even when the rain did stop shortly thereafter, play couldn't be resumed. Considering Sampras' plight at that point, it probably was just as well. The joke went around that Hillaby was a betting man and had a considerable sum riding on Sampras, thus his dive.

Sampras headed to his flat, seeking comfort from the storm of 23 Krajicek aces — to his measly five.

Thank God for Mark Hillaby.

Thursday was the Fourth of July and Sampras started off with some fireworks, holding for a 3-2 lead by aceing twice consecutively from 30-all, with a shade more spring in his step than the misty evening before.

But in the seventh game, Sampras wavered. Serving at 30-15, he double-faulted. Krajicek's inside-out forehand was a winner, with help from the net cord. On break point, a tentative Sampras served a let, then a fault. His second serve, nothing special, was returned, again, with a backhand down the line winner.

Krajicek held at love — two more aces — for 5-3. Sampras held, then braced for a last stand.

Sampras got a sniff, as he says, on the first point, a swing at a second serve, then another at a backhand pass. It landed deep. By inches. Relieved, Krajicek served and went up 30-0 with a nerveless forehand drop volley.

How's this for punctuation: ace No.30 wide, to the deuce court, followed by No.31 that went right through Sampras, who thought the ball out but never thought to argue.

One point was not the difference on this day.

It was over. A 25-match Wimbledon victory streak, a growing mystique, a chase of the legendary Borg — all gone. Sampras sounded, later, as whipped as he looked on court.

"When you play a match like this, as far as the difference, it's pretty slim," he said. "I was an inch away from winning the second set. I had a helluva lot of opportunities in the first couple of games of the match to break serve. I just didn't win the big points, and he returned and passed a lot better than I thought he would."

Slim difference? Call it minuscule. Even though Krajicek looked far superior, in reality the match turned on two converted break points and the fact that Sampras converted none of his seven break chances.

The fact that it rained on Sampras' parade didn't help either. He admitted that the delays got to him, while Krajicek coped.

"You never really feel like you're into the match," Sampras said. "You just feel like it's so sporadic, you don't have any rhythm. Tough conditions, but my hat's off to Richard.

"I was down [after losing the first two sets], disappointed, sure. But I came back out with a pretty good attitude that I was still into the match. He hit a couple of good shots to break me, and he was serving very big. And there you have it."

In a further, perhaps cathartic admission, Sampras said he felt the pressure of being a three-time champion under the gun. "He had nothing to lose …I was a little more uptight and felt the pressure a lot more."

Krajicek — who went on to beat Jason Stoltenberg in the semis and Mal Washington in the final, overpowering both just as he did Sampras — said the first rain delay, at 2-2 in the first set, helped calm him down.

"I think perhaps only in the first four games Pete was the better player," said Krajicek, the first Dutchman to win a Grand Slam title, the first non-seed to win Wimbledon since Becker in 1985.

"The first four games I was a little bit nervous; it was the first time in three years that I was on Centre Court again and then I had a whole night to think about being up two sets. So I felt some pressure myself. But the pressure was [really] on him. We were 2-2 [lifetime] before this match and I knew I could beat him."

Few people have a career edge on Sampras. Krajicek has had success beating Sampras at his own style. "I notice if I keep attacking him he starts to miss," Krajicek said. "He can hit great passing shots but you just have to keep going at him because he's such a dominant player. If I stay back, I have the feeling, off the ground, he is going to start moving me around and put pressure on me and then I have no chance. I have to come in a lot to make him hit the passing shot, put the pressure on. If you don't do that he's going to be all over you."

Pete Fischer, watching the match at home on television in California, saw the same Pete Sampras he had against Kafelnikov in the French, the one who failed to 'show up'.

The whole thing did go down incredibly easy. The sense of resignation in Sampras' voice afterward, a very troubling sign.

"I just felt it was slipping away," he said. "I just felt my time had come."

Tom Gullikson was there, watching as he had the year before but staying silent. There would be no exhortations of 'Pistol' this time. The Gullikson voice, so helpful the year before, would be better to stay muffled.

"I didn't want to say too much; I didn't want to trigger anything," Tom said.

Sampras, it appeared, had asked too much of himself in the aftermath of Gullikson's death. Running on emotion to start, running on empty too soon.

"He's definitely affected by it still, no question," Tom Gullikson said.

As was the brother, now left behind. Wimbledon 1996 could have been such a celebration for the Gulliksons, had Tim only lived that long. Tim had missed the 1995 tournament, missed his 20th Wimbledon as either a player or coach.

But 1996 was to be Tom's 20th Wimbledon.

"Tim said he sat out last year so we could celebrate our 20th Wimbledon together," Tom said at the time. "Although that's not possible I feel he's with me in spirit. I can feel his presence here, because Wimbledon was always his favourite tournament."

Pain aside, there were more straightforward, unarguable reasons that could be found for Sampras' failure to get by Krajicek, and for his uneven results during all of the 1996 season, Tom thought.

"Talking to Pete a little bit at Wimbledon, we talked about one of the keys to winning there or at any major tournament is good preparation, and Pete hasn't been able to prepare properly for any of the majors in 1996 [prior to the US Open]," Tom said.

"At the Australian he didn't get any matches in on Rebound Ace, and then he got sick. So he didn't have a good base of conditioning and got bounced by Philippoussis. Then, prior to the French, is when Tim was severely ill."

"But did anybody expect him to lose at Wimbledon?" Fischer asks.

"No. I didn't."

Neither did Sampras.

"This place has been so good to me," Sampras said. "During the past three years I'd won so many closer matches. It just didn't happen for me.

"It's hard to swallow sometimes. I put so much emphasis on Wimbledon and all the other majors that it's hard to get over a match you felt like you were in. But you're not going to win every time out there and that certainly was the case for me this time.

"My dream always was to win Wimbledon once. I never really expected to win it three times in a row. It just happened. But I have nothing to be ashamed about. I can walk out feeling I played pretty well this year. I ran into a player who was very hot and played very well. Losing to someone like that on grass… you just have to accept it sometimes.

"It's not the end of the world."

Wimbledon Record: Pete Sampras

It took Pete Sampras several years to learn the grass-court game, whereupon he took off winning 25 consecutive matches at Wimbledon between 1993-96, the best run since Bjorn Borg won five consecutive titles and 41 consecutive matches between 1976-81.

Wimbledon Record

1989

First round	Lost to Todd Woodbridge	7-5, 7-6, 5-7, 6-3

1990

First round	Lost to Christo Van Rensburg	7-6, 7-5, 7-6

1991

First round	Defeated Danilo Marcelino	6-1, 6-2, 6-2
Second round	Lost to Derrick Rostagno	6-4, 3-6, 7-6, 6-4

1992

First round	Defeated Andrei Cherkasov	6-1, 6-3, 6-3
Second round	Defeated Todd Woodbridge	7-6, 7-6, 6-7, 6-4
Third round	Defeated Scott Davis	6-1, 6-0, 6-2
Fourth round	Defeated Arnaud Boetsch	6-3, 7-5, 7-6
Quarter-finals	Defeated Michael Stich	6-3, 6-2, 6-4
Semi-finals	Lost to Goran Ivanisevic	6-7, 7-6, 6-4, 6-2

WIMBLEDON RECORD

1993

First round	Defeated Neil Borwick	6-7, 6-3, 7-6, 6-3
Second round	Defeated Jamie Morgan	6-4, 7-6, 6-4
Third round	Defeated Byron Black	6-4, 6-1, 6-1
Fourth round	Defeated Andrew Foster	6-1, 6-2, 7-6
Quarter-finals	Defeated Andre Agassi	6-2, 6-2, 3-6, 3-6, 6-4
Semi-finals	Defeated Boris Becker	7-6, 6-4, 6-4
Final	Defeated Jim Courier	7-6, 7-6, 3-6, 6-3

1994

First round	Defeated Jared Palmer	7-6, 7-5, 6-3
Second round	Defeated Richey Reneberg	6-3, 6-4, 6-2
Third round	Defeated Chuck Adams	6-1, 6-2, 6-4
Fourth round	Defeated Daniel Vacek	6-4, 6-1, 7-5
Quarter-finals	Defeated Michael Chang	6-4, 6-1, 6-3
Semi-finals	Defeated Todd Martin	6-4, 6-4, 3-6, 6-3
Final	Defeated Goran Ivanisevic	7-6, 7-6, 6-0

1995

First round	Defeated Karsten Braasch	7-6, 6-7, 6-4, 6-1
Second round	Defeated Tim Henman	6-2, 6-3, 7-6
Third round	Defeated Jared Palmer	4-6, 6-4, 6-1, 6-2
Fourth round	Defeated Greg Rusedski	6-4, 6-3, 7-5
Quarter-finals	Defeated Shuzo Matsuoka	6-7, 6-3, 6-4, 6-2
Semi-finals	Defeated Goran Ivanisevic	7-6, 4-6, 6-3, 4-6, 6-3
Final	Defeated Boris Becker	6-7, 6-2, 6-4, 6-2

1996

First round	Defeated Richey Reneberg	4-6, 6-4, 6-3, 6-3
Second round	Defeated Mark Philippoussis	7-6, 6-4, 6-4
Third round	Defeated Karol Kucera	6-4, 6-1, 6-7, 7-6
Fourth round	Defeated Cedric Pioline	6-4, 6-4, 6-2
Quarter-finals	Lost to Richard Krajicek	7-5, 7-6, 6-4

Career won-lost: 31-5

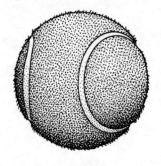

Three Wins: Sampras at Wimbledon 1993-95

Just how does one go about winning three consecutive Wimbledon titles? For starters, it generally helps to serve big. And in the 1990s, with more players than ever doing just that — making service breaks precious on grass — proficiency in tie-breakers is vital. During Sampras' 1993-95 run, he had both bases covered.

Year	Aces	Break points saved	Service games won
1993	106	14 of 22	115 of 123
1994	113	19 of 22	103 of 106
1995	106	27 of 35	124 of 132
Totals	325	60 of 79 (.759)	324 of 361 (.947)

Between 1993-95 at Wimbledon, Sampras:

    Played five matches without facing a break point;

    Won 63 of 74 sets played;

    Won 13 of 17 tie-breakers played;

    Was extended to five sets only twice.

Source: ATP Tour statistics.

Wimbledon Titles Modern Era

Pete Sampras is equal third with four other players in the modern era for the most Wimbledon titles, but he is only the third player in the modern era to have won at least three titles consecutively.

Name	Number of Titles	Years
Bjorn Borg	5	(1976–80)
Rod Laver	4	(1961–62, 1968–69)
Pete Sampras	3	(1993-95)
Boris Becker	3	(1985-86, 1989)
John McEnroe	3	(1981, 1983-84)
John Newcombe	3	(1967 1970-71)
Fred Perry	3	(1934-36)

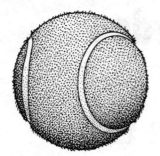

Grand Slam Singles Titles

In a very short time, Sampras has placed himself in the thick of the all-time Grand Slam mix, and it looks as if he has a good chance to eventually overtake record-holder Roy Emerson.

GRAND SLAM SINGLES TITLES

Name	Number of Titles	Place and Year
Roy Emerson	12	Australian 1961, 1963-67; French 1963, 1967; Wimbledon 1964-65; US 1961, 1964
Rod Laver	11	Australian 1960, 1962, 1969; French 1962, 1969; Wimbledon 1961-62, 1968-69; US 1962, 1969
Bjorn Borg	11	French 1974-75, 1978-81; Wimbledon 1976-80
Bill Tilden	10	Wimbledon 1920-21, 1930; US 1920-25, 1929
Pete Sampras	9	Australian 1994, 1997; Wimbledon 1993-95; US 1990, 1993, 1995, 1996
Fred Perry	8	Australian 1934; French 1935; Wimbledon 1934-36; US 1933-34, 1936
Jimmy Connors	8	Australian 1974; Wimbledon 1974, 1982; US 1974, 1976, 1978, 1982-83
Ken Rosewall	8	Australian 1953, 1955, 1971-72; French 1953, 1968; US 1956, 1970
Ivan Lendl	8	Australian 1989-90; French 1984, 1986-87; US 1985-87
John Newcombe	7	Australian 1973, 1975; Wimbledon 1967, 1970-71; US 1967, 1973
Mats Wilander	7	Australian 1984-85, 1988; French 1982, 1985, 1988; US 1988
John McEnroe	7	Wimbledon 1981, 1983-84; US 1979-81, 1984
Henri Cochet	7	French 1926, 1928, 1930, 1932; Wimbledon 1927-29
Rene Lacoste	7	French 1925, 1927, 1929; Wimbledon 1925, 1928; US 1926-27

As of February 1997.

Pete Sampras' Career Titles

As of February 1997, Pete Sampras had won 43 professional tournaments in a career that started in February 1988, with his first title coming two years later.

Year	Titles Won
1990	Philadelphia, Manchester, US Open, Grand Slam Cup
1991	Los Angeles, Indianapolis, Lyon, ATP World Championships
1992	Philadelphia, Kitzbuhel, Cincinnati, Indianapolis, Lyon
1993	Sydney, Lipton, Tokyo, Hong Kong, Wimbledon, US Open, Lyon, Antwerp
1994	Sydney, Australian Open, Indian Wells, Lipton, Osaka, Tokyo, Italian Open, Wimbledon, Antwerp, ATP World Championships
1995	Indian Wells, Queen's Club, Wimbledon, US Open, Paris Indoor
1996	San Jose, Memphis, Hong Kong, Tokyo, Indianapolis, US Open.
1997	Australian Open

Total as of February 1997: 43

Epilogue

THERE is a story that says much about Sampras' sense of tennis history, about him practising one afternoon while simultaneously spouting the number of major titles various players had won, like a kid talking baseball batting averages during the heat of a summer pennant race while knocking a ball about in the neighbour's backyard.

Too bad tennis trade cards never made it. If they had, Sampras would probably have a box full of cards tucked away in his attic, with a head full of tales stored in a mind full of tennis memories and possibilities.

"Hey, I'll trade you two Rosewalls for one Connors!...

What'ya mean, no go? Connors beat him twice in 1974. Sure, Rosewall was in the veteran stage by then, but Connors, he was the best!"

Sampras could be the best.

Eventually. Long way to go, though.

The winner of nine major titles, he trails Roy Emerson's all-time record by three. Sampras being only 25, though, Emmo is within reach.

But is the nebulous designation of 'best ever'? There is, after all, the little matter of Laver and his two real-deal Grand Slams that loom even larger than Emerson's semi-inflated — via six Australian Open titles — overall mark.

"Right now I have Pete sixth on my all-time list and he can only move up," says Pete Fischer, the former coach who likes the older players. He has his favourite player behind Laver, Don Budge, Borg, Connors and McEnroe, in a theoretical ranking order.

There is another school of thought that moves Sampras to the head of the class right now, based on the idea that the modern athlete always is superior to those of the previous era. Think about it the next time you see a clip of 1960s or 1970s tennis; try to imagine those players coping with the power and the athleticism of Sampras — or just about any of the 1990s' top 100 men.

Along those lines, aren't nine Grand Slam tournament titles in the 1990s the equivalent of 15 or 20 from a previous era?

No such thing nowadays as an easy first-round match. Yet, in 1962, the year Laver won the first of his two Grand Slams, Bob Hewitt, the South African doubles specialist, was No.8 in the world. German Willie Bungert was No.10.

In the 1970s and 1980s, the depth of talent increased considerably, but the tennis ball still was being patty-caked by today's graphite-power standards. Big servers existed, sure: Roscoe Tanner, Phil Dent and John Newcombe for starters, but such across-the-board power as seen today was unheard of.

What it comes down to, then, is this, pure and simple: In a perfect world where all tennis players from all eras would reunite for a tournament, with everyone at their absolute best, wouldn't Sampras beat them all?

If he isn't the best ever, then who is?

"I think he's certainly way up there [already]," said Rod Laver. "His game is very sound and that's the most important thing. In the modern game you just don't dominate [like in my day]. There are too many good players.

"Pete's got a good forehand and a great serve, first and second. His volleying ability is good, and he has good anticipation around the net. I think he needs to work on his backhand a little more, though. He has a certain action to it that works fine when he's confident. When he's not confident it lets him down.

"I root for him. I've very happy he recognises the older players like myself and the fact that he wants to emulate our records in the modern day. Pete's goal is to win a lot of Grand Slam tournaments; you always have to have goals to challenge your potential. But Pete's already recognised as a great player."

Tennis magazine's senior writer, Pete Bodo, is on the fence regarding Sampras' all-time stature. It can improve, Bodo figures, but it also could easily stall out. But best ever? Bodo sounds doubtful.

"We're far from being able to speculate about that; I think [such speculation] is really premature," he said. "You have to take a very empirical approach. Right now, Emerson and Laver …you have to count those Grand Slam titles [as meaningful]. I feel like when [your numbers] are in the ballpark with them, then you can start splitting hairs."

Sampras winning the French Open is also a prerequisite, Bodo feels.

"Winning each of the Grand Slam tournaments once — you have to have that," Bodo said. "The big danger [for Sampras' future] is what type of motivation he'll have [in the long term].

"In the old days the players [didn't have that problem]. They were really proud of what they did. They had a routine. They really appreciated the life they had.

"Pete certainly has a chance to be the greatest player of all time. But it's very hard to put him up there with a Grand Slam winner."

"I think he can be one of the best ever," Tom Gullikson said. "The way he plays is so natural and easy. When you hit 1,000 aces a year the game is easier. And he handles his outside responsibilities as the No.1 so well."

Joe Brandi coached Sampras before Tim Gullikson, during the 1990-91 seasons. Brandi, a long-time instructor at Nick Bollettieri's tennis academy in Bradenton, Florida, helped get Sampras' career rolling. After a six-week trial training regimen at Bollettieri's, Sampras headed to the Australian Open in January 1990 and reached the fourth round, losing to Yannick Noah. Soon after, Brandi signed on and they really went to work.

Service return, first volley, backhand slice and shot selection —

those were Sampras' weaknesses, Brandi recalls. "He's improved on all four of those areas, and that's why he's the great champion he is today," Brandi said.

"It feels good [to look back]. I contributed something."

Brandi also thinks Sampras must have a French Open title to be considered as the best. And, like Bodo, he thinks he'll get it.

"He's done well and I'm sure he'll do even better in the future," Brandi said.

The summer of 1996 began a new phase of life for Sampras. Free from the emotional burden he carried in Europe, he returned home to Tampa, to start adjusting to life without Tim Gullikson. A planned Olympics appearance was cancelled when Sampras injured his right Achilles tendon jogging in Lake Tahoe, where he was playing a celebrity golf tournament.

After a week of resting his latest injury, Sampras resumed training in hopes of regaining top form in time for the US Open.

"Hard courts are his best surface," Tom Gullikson said. "He's got all summer to prepare for the Open."

"That's where I want to be playing my best tennis." Sampras said during his Euro-swing, making no bones about the Olympics being secondary to Flushing Meadow.

The question, for the immediate future, is how much Sampras will want to play his best tennis, or if he'll want to play, period. After all, at the age of 25 — as of August 12, 1996 — he was ahead of schedule in his race with history.

He hasn't had a truly drastic slump, only valleys here and there, since he won that memorable first US Open; he could easily rationalise a rest, or even an extended hiatus if he feels it necessary.

Thing is, Sampras strives to improve.

"I'm still trying to add things to my game," he said. "I'm trying to chip-and-charge more, be a little more aggressive with my kind of style; serve-and-volley more on the second serve. I'm trying to add things to make sure I'm not predictable. And sure, I can hit every shot a little bit better.

"There are times that if I'm not playing well, my reputation will help out as far as guys will get tight if they're serving for the match or having match points. I've learned over the years just to hang in there at that moment because anything can happen. I think that's the one thing I've improved a little bit on, getting competitive and staying 'in there' mentally.

"I'm hoping one day to be in the history books. That's what I'm aiming for."

He already is. A legend, at the age of 25.

The legend goes beyond tennis already, just as it did with his idols. Sampras is a champion good guy. He gets along with media, makes friends with some of them even, another throwback to the old days. In 1995, a week before leaving for his European disaster, Sampras agreed to pose for a promotional shot, for the *Tampa Tribune*. The picture had Sampras reading a copy of the newspaper reporting on his 1994 Wimbledon victory. Sampras sat through 20 minutes of sweat-soaked posing, until the shot was right, without the first complaint.

He takes his friendships seriously. Frankie Marchesini is a friend. The 59-year-old Tampa restaurateur served Sampras a plate of pasta four years ago, and a close, father-son type relationship ensued.

They play golf — Sampras, originally reclusive when he moved to Tampa, now belongs to three clubs. They combine for charity tennis functions at Marchesini's house. And they talk. About life. About the future.

"Pete calls me his second father, but I've never wanted to be like his father," Marchesini said. "I just wanted to be his friend. But I tell you, I'd be so proud to have a kid like him.

"He'd do anything for me, I think. Sometimes I'll get a big [surprise] package from Nike, full of tennis [stuff]. Once, he gave me 15 racquets, the kind that he uses, and they were signed by him. He told me to distribute them how I liked."

Sampras is universally liked, or at least respected, among his rivals, even those who can never be considered true peers.

A story: Another professional who lives in Tampa, Mark Keil, beat Sampras in 1991 at Queen's Club. Keil is a doubles specialist whose best singles ranking was No.167 and he has won one career Grand Slam tournament singles match. These points have not been lost on Sampras.

"If you put in the paper that I lost to Mark Keil, I'll never talk to you again as long as I live — I'm serious," Sampras joked with a reporter last year who reminded him of the loss.

"Whenever he sees me, in the locker room or at a tournament, he'll say, 'You're my worst loss'," Keil said. "He's just kidding, but that's the kind of guy he is. He'll screw with you."

Sampras also is the kind of guy who'll invite Mark Keil to join him for breakfast at a Tampa restaurant, when he notices Keil sitting alone.

"A good guy," Keil said.

So good that it's just about impossible to find anybody with truly harsh words aimed directly at Sampras. In fact, you have to go back to the 1991 US Open and his 'relieved' reaction to losing, to hear somebody really go after him.

Muster made his blanket indictment of top American players early in 1996 when the No.1 controversy peaked, but Agassi was the primary target; Sampras got caught in the line of fire. Courier, the old Saddlebrook training partner who clearly is tiring of losing to Sampras, tip-toed on the edge of criticism after their French Open quarter-final, implying that Sampras' fatigued look was part façade. It came across as a small portion of sour grapes, but Courier quickly reversed himself and made sure to credit Sampras' heart instead of alleged gamesmanship.

The depth of respect that Sampras commands is best evidenced by Agassi. He is Sampras' main rival — at least he was before his mid-1996 slump — *and* his principal admirer. Agassi doesn't seem to be interested merely in Nike sales when he talks about Sampras.

"I enjoy playing Pete, just based on what he represents to me as a professional athlete," Agassi said. "Pete has definitely made me a better player and has made me realise my potential in a lot of ways. I always feel like I need to go to a different level against Pete.

EPILOGUE

"He's also taken two Grand Slam titles from me."

Sampras' character, his unfailing tendency to be a 'good guy', pleases his old coach, Fischer, nearly as much as tournament titles.

"That's very important [to me]," Fischer said. "You'll never be embarrassed to be involved with a guy like Pete Sampras.

"It's been fun. It's been a ride."

The ride, likely, will continue a while longer as Sampras tends to unfinished business.

The legend, already considerable, remains in the works.

Postscript 1:
US Open 1996

WINNING Wimbledon saved the 1995 season for Sampras. Only a fourth US Open title could save 1996.

How unlikely that looked, as Sampras left London in July, then strained his Achilles tendon and withdrew from the Olympics.

That injury was legitimate, by the way. Sampras' good friend in Tampa, Frankie Marchesini, vouched for that.

As soon as he could, Sampras was back at it, on the Saddlebrook Resort hard courts, at home with personal trainer Todd Snyder. His pre-Open tournament schedule was light, but significant: consecutive events in Cincinnati and Indianapolis, the former — the ATP Championships — part of the Mercedes Super 9 Series.

Agassi defended his title in Cincinnati, following up his Olympic gold medal and suddenly, without warning, he was in the US Open hunt once more.

Sampras went out in the quarters to Thomas Enqvist. Not much to it, either: 6-3, 6-3. Small consolation was that Enqvist also had bounced Krajicek in the round of 16.

On to Indy, where Agassi got a bye, then said bye. Leading Daniel Nestor 6-1, 2-3, Agassi got into a dispute with chair umpire Dana Loconto, taking his increasing penchant for vulgarity

— consensus is his language is out of hand, even on the practice court where he has no problem spewing filth while young fans watch — too far.

"Fuck you, Dana" was the offence. Loconto called for ATP Tour supervisor Mark Darby, who appeared and then also was cursed by Agassi. Darby tossed him from the tournament. The problem was that the magic word was directed at Loconto, rather than just uttered in a moment of tension.

So, with Agassi gone and the great rivalry on hold for yet another week, Sampras went about the business of winning a tournament. His tight 7-6 (7-3), 7-5 victory in the final over Goran Ivanisevic indicated that he, like his rival, was rounding into form in the nick of time.

Sampras' third Indy title, his fifth title of 1996, was his first since April, in Asia.

"I felt pretty good this week," Sampras said. "There were moments [in the tournament] that I played real well and moments that I wasn't there. I feel like I can get better."

Can that last quote.

It was a seven-word preview of the US Open.

How about that Open men's draw debacle? The United States Tennis Association showed some muscle by using the world rankings as a guide and not the law but then blundered big-time. It seems the 16 players to be seeded were added to the draw after the other 122 names were in place. That's not the way to do it, and left the USTA open to charges of adjusting the seeding order based on how the rest of the draw had turned out. There was the possibility of certain players benefiting, certain Americans especially.

So they redid the draw. Sampras still found himself destined for another early-round battle with Mark Philippoussis. "Some guys are just always in your quarter, it seems," Sampras said.

First, Sampras had to dismiss several no-names. Venezuelan Jimy Szymanski complied, winning only five games in three non-sets. Next up was Czechoslovakian Jiri Novak. In a peculiar effort considering the stage, Sampras ran hot and cold. Novak just ran. And ran. And ran. It took the world's No.1 player forever to beat the No.47: 6-1, 1-6, 6-3, 4-6, 6-4.

What an inexplicable close call, on the Open's first Friday afternoon.

Sampras said later he never imagined he would lose the match, even when he was dragging through the fourth set and the Czech looked rejuvenated, primed for the upset.

"I really think my experience might have come through in the end," Sampras said. "Yeah, I was missing. I was making a lot of errors. I had periods when I was pressing too much. That's the way I play. I always feel like if you keep on going for it, eventually you're going to connect on a few. That's the way I was taught and that's the way I'll continue to play. Now, if I can get better at it my next match…"

He did, and it helped his cause to have Alexander Volkov on the other side of the net. Volkov has a history of tossing it in against Sampras. He did it again, sort of, losing in three sets.

Sampras then needed to get even better. Philippoussis demands it already despite his age (19), and the lack of consistency past his serve. Sampras' strategy against him is a constant: 'Make him play'.

When that happens, when Philippoussis is forced to hit a tough volley, or hook up in virtually any sort of rally, Sampras rightfully has no fear. This time, their third match of the year and fourth overall — all in Grand Slam tournaments — Philippoussis had to 'play' from start to finish. Another straight-set victory, it easily was the most impressive of the tournament for the defending champion.

It also was overpowering enough to make most forget the image of the second-round Sampras.

Not everyone suffered memory lapse, Alex Corretja among them.

Corretja — a guy the casual fan doesn't have a clue about, who briefly surfaced in the 1995 Open when he led Agassi two sets to one, then got drummed in the last two. But the 22-year-old from

Barcelona returned to New York ranked 31st in the world, part of an imposing male Spanish contingent. Coming into the Open, six Spaniards resided in the world top 50, with Corretja the lowest-ranked of the group that did not include the two-time French Open champion Sergi Bruguera, whose fallen ranking is due to injuries, time off the tour and a struggling comeback that year.

These guys can play, and many spend a lot of time practising on Barcelona hard courts — at the complex used for the 1992 Olympics — instead of red clay as many might assume. Stylish baseliners basically, most have ample all-court skills, except perhaps for Alberto Berasategui and his unusual frying-pan forehand.

Sampras was 2-0 against Corretja, both wins on red clay of all things. Sampras also had a non-counting walkover victory, when Corretja withdrew from the 1996 Champions Cup.

Names, numbers, reason — all were out of place on a muggy Thursday afternoon that turned into a tension-filled night within a National Tennis Center stadium court that was approximately three-quarters full. Empty seats. No big deal. Outside the centre, fans were selling good tickets for face value, figuring it a perfect time to blow off the day session. It was an assumption based on the names and numbers involving Sampras-Corretja.

It was an assumption that was, well, reasonable.

Who would have thought that the names, separated by achievement and destiny, would work in concert to create more numbers. All one really need know is that four hours and eight minutes after the battle began, it raged on. At the 4:09 mark, it finally wilted. Corretja double-faulted, a second serve deep by two feet, giving Sampras the fifth-set tie-break that capped this overall score: 7-6 (7-5), 5-7 5-7 6-4, 7-6 (9-7).

Sampras spent most of the last set doing a tennis version of dead man walking. Dead man shuffling? That was it. A shuffle, from point to point, end to end, side to side. And during points, when Sampras started giving up on some shots, memories jarred. This fifth set looked strikingly akin to one Sampras played two years earlier on the same court against another foreign backboard. Jaime

Yzaga, though, had beaten Sampras. Alex Corretja walked away knowing his claim to fame for the time being would be as the man who made Sampras puke.

Fifth-set tie-break, 1-1. Sampras had gone from bad to worse, and avoided the service line, instead pacing aimlessly several feet behind it. Pausing, he bent at the waist, his body heaving as he vomited. A ball-kid ran out with a towel to clean up the mess, and Sampras somehow won the next point.

Corretja, looking as fresh as Sampras looked finished, had a match point on his racquet. Sampras served at 7-8, and had to stretch wide right to track down, then guide with a forehand volley, a Corretja forehand.

Sampras had two match points, losing the first at 6-5 by netting a forehand. The second was set up by a remarkable 90mph second-serve ace wide — untouchable — to the deuce court. Next came the double-fault that brought Corretja to his knees, but only for a few seconds. He quickly scooted to net where a cursory hand-shake gave way to a warm embrace.

Victory secured, the task turned to recovery. Two days to get ready for a semi-final against Ivanisevic, who ended Stefan Edberg's last Grand Slam tournament in the quarters and was having his best-ever Open.

Recovery started immediately. Sampras couldn't attend the post-match interview. Dehydrated and cramping, he was given two litres of fluid intravenously. That helped his body. Only time could help his heart, which was broken again after the match when he tearfully told his girlfriend that the late Tim Gullikson "got me through that one."

Snyder went to work doing what he could. Sampras got a massage to reduce the lactic acid build-up in his muscles and lessen the soreness sure to set in. Snyder concentrated on the body, hoping heart and soul would jump on board. There ensued a carefully calculated plan of nutrition and exercise, one eased by avoiding the National Tennis Center completely the next day, but one that started that night in a most unlikely setting.

"We went to a diner and had some pancakes and scrambled eggs," Snyder said. "The next morning, back to the diner for pancakes and English muffins."

Then came the tricky part.

"I wanted Pete to get some exercise, but not enough to drain the body," Snyder said. "So we went out to where a friend of mine lives on Long Island. He has a court. It was nice and quiet. No hassles. And Pete had a casual one-hour hit with Paul Annacone."

The rest of the day, the high-carbohydrate stacking continued. Pasta and pizza for lunch. Same thing for dinner, but with a small portion of meat, "because you need a little protein," Snyder said.

Rejuvenated as well as possible, Sampras had the best possible semi-final opponent in Ivanisevic, whose massive serve made for short points. Just what Sampras needed. A low-maintenance match endurance-wise, requiring minimal bursts of energy.

Against Ivanisevic, Sampras uses the same simple, direct strategy as he does against Philippoussis: Dig in and make the guy hit some shots other than his serve. The strategy took Sampras to the brink of a straight-set victory. Ivanisevic, to his credit, raised his game in a third-set tie-break and survived four match points.

The second match point, though, escaped Sampras when he double-faulted at 6-5. When Ivanisevic ended the breaker with a service winner, making it 11-9, the prospect of another set had Sampras incensed.

''I had a hard time looking at anything positively after losing the tie-break," Sampras said. "I was just kind of thinking, during the first three or four games of the fourth set, how stupid I played [the match points]. But I tried to regain my composure and tried to look at it like 'well, I'm still up a set and playing pretty well'."

Well enough to forge a service break in the eighth game and close out the match.

"It was a completely different match than Corretja," Sampras said. "With Goran, it's like riding a roller-coaster. You're not sure what he's going to do."

The semi-final may have had its moments, but it paled next to the Corretja ordeal, as did the final against Sampras' boyhood rival, Michael Chang.

Chang ended Agassi's decent run in the semi-finals, but had little left for Sampras. Another straight-set victory 6-1, 6-4, 7-6 (7-3) — gave Sampras a fourth US Open title. Since 1968, when the 'open era' began, only two other men have so achieved. Jimmy Connors won five Opens, John McEnroe four.

As with the Corretja victory, though, scores and statistics told little.

The final was held on Tim Gullikson's 45th birthday. Twin brother Tom Gullikson, an integral part of the Sampras camp but in a non-coaching capacity, was on hand and celebrated inwardly, knowing this title was a tribute to Timmy.

Delaina Mulcahy talked of closure, of how Sampras might finally let go of the pain that had consumed him since Tim Gullikson's May 3 death.

"I was thinking about Tim all day today and all during the match," Sampras said. "I still felt his spirit and even though he's not with us he's still very much in my heart. I wouldn't be [a champion] if it wasn't for his help. I saw Tom when I was holding up the trophy and that was a nice moment.

"I'm just glad it's over. This definitely saved my year."

Sampras left New York a champion but on the horizon was another obstacle. After the final, Paul Annacone told members of the media that Sampras might undergo a major physical examination, aiming to pinpoint possible health problems that would explain his repeated breakdowns during matches. A week later, the *Toronto Globe and Mail* reported that Sampras may have anaemia. The reporter, freelance journalist Tom Tebbutt, cited no specific sources, which discredited the story considerably.

Sampras and his trainer Snyder declined to comment on the story, fuelling speculation that it was true. As it turned out, other sources confirmed Tebbutt's story. Anaemia is a treatable medical condition that laymen often define as a lack of iron in the blood. It is identified by an insufficient number of red corpuscles in the blood. Most people who have the condition tire easily or at least more easily than people without it.

Sampras said that no matter what, his career would not be jeopardised by his health. Perhaps not, but it could become a factor in some of the gruelling matches that lie ahead. In any case, anaemia would put to rest the contentions of Courier and Corretja, among others, that Sampras sometimes uses a façade of fatigue.

The Sampras achievements with this condition cast his Grand Slam titles in an entirely different light.

More like a glow.

Still Much to Do

ON a sultry Florida October afternoon, finally, Pete Sampras can relax. And reflect. He is having fun, only fun, for a change, back home in Tampa, hitting tennis balls without worrying how they'll come back. Most of the time, in fact, they aren't coming back.

On the other side, alternating as receivers/targets of Sampras' serves, are members of the New Jersey Nets, a miserably unsuccessful NBA team that has been holding its pre-season training camp at a nearby college, a team that has sought Sampras' counsel earlier in the week about what it takes to become a champion. The Nets are about as removed from championship contention as a professional sports team gets in America.

A friendly challenge between Sampras and the team resulted in this get-together at Saddlebrook Resort, where Sampras trains. And after only a few moments, it is clear that the Nets at last have found a sport they're worse at than basketball.

Sampras isn't serving all-out, Not even close. Doesn't matter. The balls whiz by the Nets, one by one.

Occasionally, someone gets a racquet on a ball — a racquet, not strings. Twice, Sampras nails a receiver in the crotch, then winces mischievously at the sight. Another time, a 6ft 6ins physical specimen flails at a spinning, twisting ball like a two-year-old, slips and falls flat on his ass.

A half-hour later, the serve-and-heckle session is over. Two balls have been returned, both off what would have been second serves in actual competition. The Nets have been humbled but, what the hell, they'll get used to it. Pretty soon they will have lost 15 of their first 20 games in the NBA season. They need to have some fun too.

They gather around Sampras for a photograph, their towering frames dwarfing the world's No 1 player, who stands at 6ft 1ins. Sampras laughs. He hasn't done much of that for most of 1996. It feels good. It looks good. At this moment, the trials of 1996 — an early-round Australian Open defeat, Tim Gullikson's death, humbling losses at the French Open and Wimbledon, and a five-set US Open ordeal against Alex Corretja — are forgotten.

When Sampras' career is through, it will be most interesting to see where 1996 fits in regarding the overall assessment. In that year Sampras was only 25, certain to play at least five more years, he said, certain to add to his total of eight Grand Slam tournament titles, others said. Indeed, that total quickly became nine with victory in the Australian Open in January 1997.

With time will come the perspective needed to fully judge 1996 — and to fully appreciate it. If viewed strictly in terms of wins and losses, the season will always be considered mediocre. But surely, there is no chance of such short-sightedness infringing on the year's accomplishments, which involved so much more than embellishing the record book.

And besides, Sampras points out, there *was* a bit of embellishment, here and there.

"A lot of people have been talking about how this has been a bad year for me," Sampras said. "But I got to the semis at the French Open, which I'd never done before, reached the quarter-finals at Wimbledon and then won the US Open again. It hasn't been that bad [on the court]."

Therein lies the thread of this Sampras season. More than anything else, it should forever be recalled for how it proceeded in the face of tragedy. Sampras' coach, Gullikson, died in May ending a courageous 18-month battle with brain cancer. Yet, Sampras trudged on to Europe, fashioning a stunning run at the French before losing to eventual champion Yevgeny Kafelnikov in the semi-finals. Another eventual champion, Richard Krajicek, dumped him out of Wimbledon. His fourth US Open title — highlighted by the quarter-final victory over Corretja, during which Sampras became ill on court — reminded people that he was, after all, still the world's top-ranked player. He would retain that status until the end of the year. For the fourth consecutive year, joining John McEnroe and Jimmy Connors as the only players to so dominate the men's pro tour.

As a footnote to 1996, Sampras won a third ATP Tour Championship title in mid-November in Hanover, Germany, defeating Boris Becker in an epic five-set final.

"One of the best matches I've ever been a part of," Sampras said after the 3-6, 7-6(7-5), 7-6(7-4), 6-7(11-13), 6-4 victory achieved despite overwhelming support for Becker by the German crowd.

"This is what the game is all about. It's not the money, it's the great matches. They were rooting for him, but they were not against me. It was a great atmosphere and it raises the level of tennis and it's fun to be a part of it."

Incidentally, regarding money, Sampras collected US $1.34 million, bringing his 1996 earnings to US$3,286,252, based on a won-loss record of 65-11.

As the year was winding down, as if Sampras hadn't had enough to deal with off the court, came two more revelations of a personal nature. After the US Open, the reports that he suffered from a mild form of anaemia known as thalassemia minor were confirmed by his sister Stella, coach of the UCLA women's team. But, while some suggested the thalassemia could explain his repeated endurance problems during matches, Stella, saying she also had the disease, stressed that it was no big deal and that it had played no part in her brother's conditioning shortcomings. Sampras, meanwhile, offered up repeated public denials that he had thalassemia.

And finally, there was the break-up between Sampras and his girlfriend of six years, Delaina Mulcahy. Mulcahy apparently moved out the their US$770,000 two-storey Tampa home in October. Reportedly, the split resulted from her desire to be married versus Sampras' desire to wait. That polarity had been the source of occasional public banter between the two during the previous couple of years although, on the surface, it had always seemed good-natured.

Tough year, indeed, but a champion always bounces back. As 1996 ended, Sampras was already being spotted around Tampa in the company of another woman, one apparently much younger than Delaina. He also was being spotted more frequently at Saddlebrook Resort, working harder than ever on his conditioning, sometimes twice a day.

Looking back on 1996, will always conjure up both pain and pleasure for Sampras. Looking ahead to 1997, and beyond, would be his solace. And after all, there is still much to do. In tennis. In love. In life.

Postscript 2: Australian Open 1997

T WO MONTHS prior to the 1997 Australian Open, Pete Sampras started making sure he would not go to the tournament as unprepared as the year before. Many days were spent in the company of Mike Nisharra, Director of Fitness and Conditioning at Saddlebrook Resort. Nisharra, formerly involved in training US Olympic athletes, was part of an overall upgrading of Saddlebrook's training facilities that Sampras had come to love. In November, a new 3,000 square foot, multi-million dollar centre was completed.

And so, during November, December and early January, when Sampras was not on the road, he spent a good portion of his time at Saddlebrook immersed in a newly-intensified regime. Twice-daily workouts — on and off the court — became commonplace. Sampras was eyeing Australia, and the possibility of a ninth Grand Slam title, which would bring him to within three of Roy Emerson's all-time record.

Sampras played a tune-up event at Kooyong Stadium prior to

the Australian, losing to Michael Chang, then brushing it off. He was playing well and felt he would soon be playing better. And after all, it surely did seem as if this tournament was coming to him. Agassi was out with an injury. So were two of the guys who had beaten him in the 1996 Grand Slam events — French Open champion Yevgeny Kafelnikov and Wimbledon winner Richard Krajicek. Then, in the first round, defending champion Boris Becker went down, losing to clay-courter Carlos Moya of Spain.

Suddenly, the tournament looked for all the world like it was Sampras' to lose. Then, incredibly, he almost did just that. After playing one of his most complete victories in years in allowing Aussie Mark Woodforde only two games over three sets, Sampras struggled through consecutive five-set victories, the first inexplicable because it came against a qualifier, Dominik Hrbaty. The second could be explained away. Alberto Costa, another Spaniard, is capable of beating anyone, any time.

But the sum effect of ten sets within four days was to make Sampras seem quite vulnerable, especially considering the 100-degree heat, inherent in any sweltering Aussie summer. The heat became so intense that for one day, the retractable roof at the National Tennis Centre was closed to protect both players and fans. For a day, the Australian Open had been transformed into an indoor Grand Slam.

Having escaped elimination, Sampras faced an imposing challenge in the semi-finals — Thomas Muster, who was playing some of his best hard-court tennis and crediting a new computerised approach to charting matches. Sampras scoffed at such an impersonal approach. Ever the throwback deep-down, Sampras said, "I don't try to over-complicate things."

He kept it simple against Muster, a 6-1, 7-6, 6-3 victory that was of the quality exhibited against Woodforde and, considering the competition, even more impressive.

Sixteen aces helped Sampras turn the potentially-tough match into a routine one.

"The computer is good," Muster said, "It told me exactly the right things to do, but you still have got to make the shots. Pete's the No.1 player. He's confident and he has the best all-around game. He's a Grand Slam player and I've just got to give him credit."

That was a forerunner of the accolades that poured in following the final, in which Sampras dispatched the surprising Moya (who had followed the Becker upset by beating second-seed Michael Chang in the semi-finals) 6-2, 6-3, 6-3 with a display his old coach Pete Fischer must have loved. Sampras played a tactically-perfect match, carefully mixing his power with placement, especially on serve. So many times he took a bit off his serves, catching Moya off-guard while setting up the rest of his attacking game. Moya was visibly nervous. When he wasn't being beaten, he was beating himself.

It was smart tennis by Sampras, Appropriate tennis. The Rebound Ace hard-court, baked by the sun, had grown rubbery. slower than usual. And with balls that were slightly heavier than normal, all-out power was somewhat neutralised. This was tennis that required, for Sampras, more thought than usual. He was up to it, obviously. Afterward, he sat back and enjoyed his work against Muster and Moya. "To beat these [baselining] guys in these conditions, I really surprised myself a bit," Sampras said. "This is the toughest major I think I've won so far, physically. To come through is a good effort."

"Pete is No.1 and showed it," Moya said. "In a Grand Slam final he's almost unbeatable."

Index

INDEX

INDEX

INDEX